An Introduction to Business Accounting for Managers

FIFTH EDITION

by

W. C. F. HARTLEY, F.C.A., F.C.M.A., J.Dip.M.A.
Financial Training Consultant

PERGAMON

U.K.	Elsevier Science Ltd., The Boulevard, Langford Lane, Kidlington, Oxford OX5 1GB, U.K.
U.S.A.	Elsevier Science Inc., 660 White Plains Road, Tarrytown, New York 10591-5153, U.S.A.
JAPAN	Elsevier Science Japan, Tsunashima Building Annex, 3-20-12 Yushima, Bunkyo-ku, Tokyo 113, Japan

First edition 1965
Second edition 1969
Third edition 1980
Reprinted (with corrections) 1983
Fourth edition 1987
Fifth edition 1994

Library of Congress Cataloging-in-Publication Data
Hartley, W. C. F.
An introduction to business accounting for managers,
W. C. F. Hartley—5th ed.
p.cm.
Includes index.
1. Accounting. 2. Managerial accounting
I. Title
HF5635.H335 1994
657'024658 - - dc20. 93-48264.

British Library Cataloguing-in-Publication Data
A catalogue record for this book is available from the
British Library

ISBN 0-08-042402-3 (Hardcover)
ISBN 0-08-042403-1 (Flexicover)

Printed in Great Britain by BPC Wheatons Ltd, Exeter

An Introduction to Business
Accounting for Managers

FIFTH EDITION

Related titles of interest

ANYANE-NTOW, K.
International Handbook of Accounting Education and Certification

BOYLE, D.
Strategic Service Management

BRYSON, J. M.
Strategic Planning for Public Service and Non-Profit Organizations

JONSSON, S.
Accounting for Improvement

McNAMEE, P.
Tools and Techniques for Strategic Management

Related Pergamon journals—Sample copy available on request

Accounting, Management and Information Technology
Accounting, Organizations and Society
European Management Journal
International Business Review
Journal of Accounting Education
Long Range Planning

To

F. E. B.
for inspiration

D. M. S.
for motivation

B. E. P.
for application

and

D. E. H.
for toleration

Contents

Preface to the Fifth Edition

IT WOULD be pretentious to claim that a book of this size was a complete treatise on the wide subject of Business Accounting, and I do not make such a claim. The reader will be given a taste of various aspects of the subject and, if thereby the appetite is whetted for one particular aspect, the reader will find the libraries overflowing with volumes to satiate that appetite for deeper, wider, knowledge.

This is not a textbook in accounting principles and it is not directed towards the professional accountancy student. However, that student may be interested in my approach to the subject which differs from that adopted in a strictly theoretical treatise on accounting.

The readers for whom this book is written fall into two categories:

(1) Students undertaking a course in business studies or management studies (be it a Diploma Course, a First Degree, or an MBA). These students require only a general appreciation of accounting principles and techniques. What is more important is an appreciation of the use and limitations of the accounting service they come into contact with in their business career. They require also to be able to examine critically and interpret accounting information which comes their way. I hope that in this book I have met these students' requirements which were constantly in my mind whilst the book was being compiled. Indeed, much of the material used formed the basis of lectures given to students enrolled on management and other business courses at various teaching establishments with which I have been associated.

(2) Those middle and senior non-financial managers already in business who have never had any formal financial training but who, as they are promoted, are somehow expected both to behave comfortably and competently with financial data which comes across their desk and also to play a full role at management and board meetings. If such a manager is baffled by figures or whose blood runs cold at the sight of a balance sheet, I hope this book will act as a lifeline.

Over the years since the First Edition of the book, this main objective has remained unchanged. However, the text has undergone many changes to reflect the frequently changing focus, fashion, thrust and external pressures (legal and other) which have impacted on current financial thinking and practice in industry. I hope that these textual changes have also been in step with the greater financial awareness of those non-financial managers referred to above and with the significantly improved professionalism, technical skill and computing power of practising accountants and finance managers.

My final words must be ones of thanks:

(a) to my many former non-financial colleagues in industry who, perhaps unwittingly, have been such a great help in identifying the problems that they face in dealing with this subject;

(b) to those many mature, non-financial, managers with whom I have worked on training programmes and who have made suggestions for improvements in the text;

(c) to those accountants and finance directors with whom I have worked and who have spared no effort in helping to keep my thinking and approach current and practical (they will recognise some of their own terminology or formulae in the text);

(d) to Geoff Gibson of John Waddington PLC for permission to reproduce and to quote freely from their published accounts: and

(e) to my wife Dorothy, who did not audibly complain at the many hours I have been closeted at the desk during the writing of these five editions and who was such a help during the tedious process of proof reading.

W. C. F. H.
1994

CHAPTER 1

Use and Abuse of Accounting

The Profit Motive

Why does a business exist? Different writers at different times have defined the motive force behind any business. Some claim that a business exists to provide the product or service which will satisfy a need created by the public; others claim that a business exists in order to provide means of livelihood by its employment of workers.

Whilst both these objectives may be present, neither could be fulfilled were it not for the one and all-important necessity behind any commercial business unit: the need to be financially viable. Financial viability has two aspects: (1) the need to make profit in the long term, (2) the need to generate cash flow and thus stay solvent in the short term—these two aspects are related but vastly different as we shall see later. If a business does not see financial viability as its prime objective it may not be able either to provide products and services or to keep workers in employment. Profit to a business is like food to a human body: the body must grow and develop—with the assistance of food; take away the supply of food and the body wastes away and eventually dies.

However, there are certain types of business to which the profit motive cannot apply. Business engaged in the provision of a necessary service to the community (e.g. National Health hospitals, research associations) exist for that very purpose and not for making profit. Indeed, the business may receive no direct income from the recipient of the service provided and, in these circumstances, it is impossible to make a "profit" in the full commercial sense. If this is the case, financial viability should be interpreted as the desire to provide the service as economically and efficiently as possible. Opinions are frequently expressed on the role of the nationalized industries and others receiving government aid: should these industries be motivated by profit or some other motive based on the National Interest? The writer does not wish to become involved in this discussion, and the

1

comments in this book are therefore directed to the normal commercial business motivated by profit, needing to stay solvent and operating in a free-enterprise system.

If it is established that financial viability is essential to the existence of a commercial business, it follows that there must be some system which records what is happening in the business, day by day, with a view to measuring the ultimate profit achieved. Such a system of recording and measuring is provided by the Accountant and the process is called Accounting.

Twin Fields of Accounting

Accountants go by many names: Financial Accountants, Cost Accountants, Management Accountants, to list but three. What's in a name? The accountant, whatever may be his title, is the specialist operator in his field: the field of providing a vital service to management in its pursuance of financial viability. This service has two clearly defined aspects which may in fact be regarded as twin fields of accounting.

Let us consider how a business functions. A business draws upon resources (materials, men, money and machines) from large groups outside the business (suppliers, employees and those who provide capital: on loan, e.g. banks, or as owners, e.g. shareholders). These resources are converted by the business system into finished product, goods or services which are supplied to another large group outside the business (customers). This sequence is demonstrated graphically on page 3.

Customers, one hopes, will eventually pay in cash and this cash will be used to reimburse suppliers and to pay employees, provide interest on the loan capital and leave a surplus which is profit. This profit is appropriated in three ways: part goes in taxation; part goes in the form of dividend to provide a return on owners' (shareholders) capital; part goes back down the funnel to feed the growing business. Thus the cycle is completed, cash flows round to the top of the chart and allows more resources to flow down the funnel labelled business system.

Financial Accounting

There is a commercial need, often strengthened by a legal obligation, that records be maintained to keep this flow of cash under control, e.g. to ensure that customers pay for what they have received; that those who have

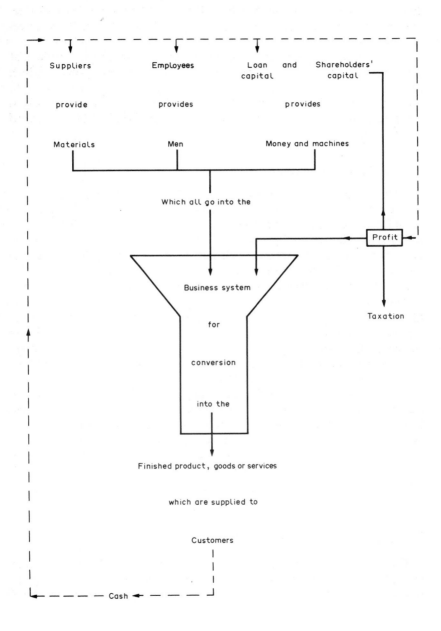

provided resources are adequately rewarded for the services they have provided, that taxation is fairly assessed. These records must be designed to show also what profit has been earned, i.e. what balance of income remains after satisfying all outgoings. This is the field of financial accounting and its records are concerned with:

_ 1. The financial relationship of the business with the *outside* world.
2. The *overall* result, in terms of profit or loss, of the activities of the business.
3. An *historical* review of what has happened.

Referring to the chart on page 3, financial accounting records all that goes on *outside* the central funnel labelled business system.

Management Accounting

There is also a second field. Management must have monetary information if it is to guide the course of business successfully. The information provided in the field of financial accounting will help up to a point but the real need is for something more detailed—detail, perhaps, in respect of individual departments, jobs, processes or projects—detail which will assist management in answering such questions as: which is our most profitable product?; is department X operating as efficiently as department Y?; should we close factory B?; should we purchase new machine Z?; will it be cheaper to purchase component N instead of manufacturing it ourselves? Note that some of this information relates to the present and the future, in addition to the past.

This quite different approach forms the field of cost, or management accounting which, referring again to the chart on page 3, amplifies what goes on *inside* the central funnel.

Management's Use of Accounting

Preparation of accounting information is not part of the manager's duties but he or she must be able to understand and interpret accounting information coming into their hands. This may appear to be a contradictory statement, but it is not: a useful comparison can be drawn between the manager and the captain of a modern jet airliner.

The captain holds in his hands a complex and expensive mechanism together with the lives of many people. He must guide his airliner along its predetermined path through day and night, good and bad weather conditions. To assist him in this task he is provided with a vast array of instruments, dials, lights, charts, sounds and messages. He is not expected to know how the instruments are constructed but he must be able to understand and interpret the message they convey. He must also know the conditions under which certain instruments may require correction when being read, but above all he must know which are the vital instruments which must be trusted and followed even when all his instincts tell him not to do so. Let it be stressed that our captain needs to know far more than instrument reading alone if he is to fly his airliner successfully; however, the ability to read instruments is an essential attribute!

Similarly our manager should learn to read accounting information, know its limitations, know when to correct a reading and when to accept one; but our manager does not need to know how to design, construct, operate or repair the accounting system.

Accounting: a Service with Limitations

Accounting is, therefore, a service to management, a special-purpose tool which must be used but not misused. Like any special-purpose tool, if it is neglected or not used it will surely go rusty and fail to provide the good service for which it was designed. However, all tools have their limitations and it is well to point out at this early stage some fundamental limitations inherent in any system of accounting.

Accounting is a language. One of the fundamental reasons for failure to understand accounting documents is the failure to realize that accounting is a language which has its own rules, so words used must be interpreted accordingly. The qualified accountant has studied this language but many non-accountants have not. The problem is complicated by the fact that many of the words used in accounting are also used in everyday, non-accounting, English language with very different meanings, "cost" and "value", for example, conjure up for the non-accountant the picture of a price tag in a shop; for the accountant they may mean something far removed from an actual cash price. This problem is very real and must be appreciated. An Englishman wishing to speak French undertakes a serious period of study, yet he automatically assumes he can speak American without any study because the words and rules are similar. However, words in English may have different meanings in American. A "public school" in American language, for instance, means one available to the public at large—what the English language understands by "public school" the Americans call a "private school". A full understanding of the English language does not equip one for an adequate understanding of either the American language or the accounting language.

Money is the common denominator. Any one system must adopt a common unit of measurement. Accounting has selected money value as its unit of measurement. Therefore the day-to-day transactions of business, undertaken in many different units of measurement, have all to be converted to money values.

This gives rise to two major shortcomings:

1. Accounting can never give a complete picture because some events defy expression in monetary terms and must therefore be omitted. A picture presented by an accountant will not tell you, for example, that your sales manager and works manager are not on speaking terms or that your competitor has developed a better product than yours. These two pieces of information are vital to the management of a business but an accounting system must ignore them.

2. A common misconception when reading accounting documents is that the value placed on any item by the accountant represents what that item is worth in today's money value: as a general rule the only item to which this applies is cash in hand or on deposit at short call. Accounting traditionally has added together dissimilar money value items. With the passage of time money values change but, under the language of accounting, the value placed upon any item is *not necessarily* expressed in terms of today's value of money. If the Historical Cost Accounting Convention is used, included in the calculation of profit may be wages paid for at today's value and a proportion of the original cost of a building purchased many years ago when the £ was worth perhaps twice what it is worth today. However, if the Current Cost Accounting Convention is used, some or all of these items may have been converted so as to reflect current replacement values or present-day money values.

The difference between the historical cost and current cost accounting conventions is fundamental to an understanding of financial information and will be explained in greater detail later.

Figures may be approximations. Once a figure is committed to paper by an accountant, it is commonly accepted with an air of accuracy that was never intended by the accountant. All units of measurement have degrees of approximation; the unit of measurement used in accounting is no exception.

The dimension of the paper on which this printing appears can be measured with a substantial degree of accuracy; the distance this book has travelled from the publisher to you can be less accurately measured; whereas the distance from here to the sun can only be very approximately measured. Similarly in accounting; the cash in the till can be accurately measured but many other items can at best be only approximations.

This does not detract from the value of accounting information, provided the user appreciates the degree of approximation incorporated in the result. After all: you need only an approximate idea of the distance from *A* to *B* if you wish to forecast the time the journey will take.

Figures may reflect opinions. Individual accountants, like members of other professional bodies, hold their own opinions which are reflected in the figures they produce. In particular, opinions may vary over the money value to be used or the degree of approximation to be tolerated. Furthermore, accountants are, by nature, conservative in their outlook and will, therefore, often anticipate losses but seldom take account of profits until they have been earned. Accountants cannot detail every little item and those happenings which are considered to be of no material effect may be ignored. Thus it is not inconceivable that two accountants, who hold different opinions, may produce two different sets of figures out of the same basic information—just as two doctors may differ in their diagnosis of the same symptoms displayed by a patient.

Time is an artificial compartment. If someone were to ask you the cost of operating your motor car for a period of 6 months, how would you answer? You would find it impossible to calculate an accurate cost until the car had been sold and the loss on capital outlay known: you will therefore have to estimate this loss during the 6 months. Suppose you bought new tyres during this 6-month period: is the whole cost of the tyres to be included in the running cost for the 6 months or a part only? If so, which part?

Similarly, the true profit of a firm can be accurately measured only when the firm finally goes out of business. This, of course, is no good to management who require financial information on the results of operating different parts of the business and require it at frequent intervals—annually, quarterly, monthly or for some other period of time. We have seen above that figures may be approximations or reflect opinions, but the position is aggravated by the creation of these iron compartments of time. Business is a continuing function and yet the accountant must assume that an iron curtain falls at two dates when assets must be valued and between which income and expenditure must be assessed. The whole concept of dividing time into compartments is thus artificial.

Figures tell one story at once. The "language barrier" of accounting was referred to above. Arising partly from this, there is a widely held belief that figures are scientific facts which are good in any circumstances or conditions. Such is not the case; a figure is valid for the special purpose for which it was created and only in special circumstances will it still be true in general application.

Three different valuations may be placed upon a piece of equipment depending on whether the valuation is required for assessing profit, or for fire insurance cover, or for attempting a sale. Each of these figures will be true in its own special circumstances.

A different figure of "cost of producing product X" should be expected depending on whether the figure were required as a useful historical fact or as a basis for an expansion programme or in deciding whether to make or buy product X.

Thus when considering any figure one must always bear in mind the purpose for which it was prepared.

Another aspect of this same problem will be seen when considering the general accounting routines of the business. These routines have been devised to produce automatically the specific accounting information required by management. This is the story the figures tell and to expect them to tell another story may be expecting the accountant to unscramble an omelette. Accounting routines can of course be altered to enable a new story to be told—but then do not expect the old story as well!

The Reliability of the Accounting Service

All these inherent limitations must be appreciated when using the accounting service. The accounting service was referred to earlier as a tool—all tools have their limitations beyond which the tool should not be used or its relative efficiency will be impaired. But this does not detract from the real usefulness of that tool. Similarly in accounting: the service is still useful and is quite reliable—if its limitations in use are appreciated. In particular, financial accounting provides the following vital information without which a business cannot be managed successfully:

1. The profit or loss arising from the business and the source of such profit or loss.

2 The cash flow (positive or negative) generated by the business and the source and use of such cash flow.

3 The capital employed in the business and the nature and value of all the property and possessions of the business, which will reveal:

    (a) what is owned by the business

    (b) what is owing to the business and by whom

    (c) what is owing by the business and to whom

    (d) the financial position of the business at any point in time.

Management accounting provides further, equally vital and more detailed information which will be discussed in a later chapter.

CHAPTER 2

Development and Principles of Book-keeping

IN CHAPTER 1 we established that there is need for some system of recording the monetary aspect of day-to-day business transactions. The purpose of this chapter is to trace the development of these systems and to examine the principles of operating the system most commonly in use today. Let it be clearly understood that there is no one "system of accounting" good for all businesses and for all time. A business accounting system is rather like a suit—every suit has the same features: jacket, sleeves, buttons, etc., but no one suit will appeal to or fit everyone. Some suits can be bought "off the peg" and may require slight alteration while others are specially made to measure. Pattern and quality of cloth and "cut" vary considerably. As a person grows older, contours change and the suit ceases to fit or wears out, so it is time to discard the old suit and buy a new one. Similar principles apply to a business accounting system.

Brief History of Accounting

One of the first accounts of recorded transactions dates back to the year 2285 B.C. in Babylon: "Article 104—If a trader has given his agent Corn, Wool, Oil or any merchandise to sell, the agent must write down their value on a sealed document which is given to the trader."

Examination of Egyptian papyrus scrolls has revealed careful records of income and expenditure, the Ancient Greeks developed a crude clearing-house system and early Roman records show signs of household accounts.

Early English business transactions were recorded by means of a "tally stick". Notches were cut in a stick (indicating the transaction which had taken place) which was then split, each party taking one half. The halves were married together at time of settlement.

In the twelfth and thirteenth centuries, Venetian merchants originated a system of accounting which was to become a standard international system—Double-entry Book-keeping. This was first written up in 1494 by a Franciscan monk—Luca Pacioli.

Double-entry Book-keeping

Any business transaction can be considered from two distinct points of view. If I buy a motor car for £1000 cash, two things have happened: I have gained a car and lost £1000 cash. Similarly from the point of view of the man who sold me the car: he has gained £1000 cash but lost a car. So every business transaction has two aspects and the double entry system records *both* aspects (Americans refer to this as the Dual Aspect System).

Double entry book-keeping has been defined as "that system by which every transaction involving a transfer of money or money's worth is recorded in two separate accounts forming part of a series, not merely by way of repetition, but so as to record the two distinct aspects in which every such transaction is capable of being regarded".

The Account

In the above definition the word "account" was used. This is the basic accounting record and in a traditional book-keeping system an account is opened for every classification of business transaction which we wish to record. The form on which the account is prepared is shown below.

NAME OF ACCOUNT

Date	Details	Ref.	£.	Date	Details	Ref.	£.
	Debit side Value of items coming in				*Credit side* Value of items going out		

The name of the account appears at the top of the page. On the left-hand side (the debit side) are recorded items coming into the account and on the right-hand side (the credit side) are recorded items going out.

In the details column is put the name of the account completing the double entry series and the account (or page) number of the completing account appears in the reference column to assist cross-reference.

For simplicity of demonstration in this book an abbreviated form of account in the shape of a letter "T" will be used, as will the following standard abbreviations: A/c—account; Dr—debit; Cr—credit.

The earlier transaction of buying a car would be recorded thus: Dr Car A/c £1000 (reflecting gain of a car—value coming in) Cr Cash A/c £1000 (reflecting loss of cash—value going out) and would appear in the accounts as follows:

Car A/c			Cash A/c	
£	£		£	£
Cash 1000				Car 1000
i.e. value coming into this A/c from cash			i.e. value going out of this A/c on a car	

However, the man who sold the car would make up the following accounts:

Car A/c			Cash A/c	
£	£		£	£
	Cash 1000		Car 1000	

Cash and Credit Transactions

In the above example cash was handed over immediately in exchange for the car: this is known as a cash transaction. However, the car may have been received on trust and cash paid, say, a month later: this is known as a credit transaction. Book-keeping regards a credit transaction as two separate transactions and makes two sets of entries thus:

Transaction 1:	Dr Car A/c	£1000 (value coming into this A/c)
	Cr J. Jones A/c	£1000 (value going out of this A/c)
	(supplier of car)	
Transaction 2:	Dr J. Jones A/c	£1000 (value coming into this A/c)
	Cr Cash A/c	£1000 (value going out of this A/c)

which will be recorded thus:

Car A/c			J. Jones A/c	
£	£		£	£
J. Jones 1000			Cash 1000	Car 1000
(Transaction 1)			(Transaction 2)	(Transaction 1)

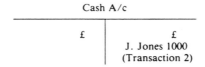

Classification of Accounts

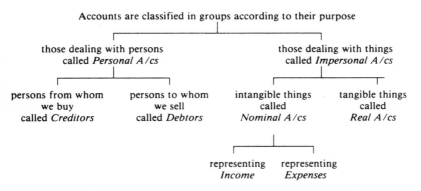

For accounting purposes, accounts are classified in groups according to their purpose. The chart above shows this classification, the significance of which will become apparent in later reading.

Books of Account

The one essential book of account is the *ledger*, a book wherein are recorded on separate pages the accounts which it is deemed necessary to open in order to obtain the desired amount of detail of the business transactions. As a business grows, more and more accounts will be required and it is common practice to subdivide the ledger into separate books to avoid creating one cumbersome ledger. This also permits several clerks to work on the ledger simultaneously. The following are subdivisions generally in use:

1. Personal A/cs are included in a *personal ledger* or alternatively creditors and debtors A/cs are separated in a *purchase ledger* and a *sales ledger* respectively.

2. One particular real A/c itself is very bulky, namely the cash A/c, which appears on its own as a *cash book*.

3. The ledger containing the remaining accounts is variously called the *impersonal*, *nominal* or *private ledger*.

In addition to classifying transactions by type in ledger accounts, accountants often wish to keep a record of transactions by groups in chronological order day by day. Books used for this purpose are called *day books* or *journals*. As with ledgers, there may be several day books—for example, a chronological record of sales would form a *sales day book* and of purchases a *purchase day book*. These books are mentioned briefly to complete the picture but are not important for the purposes of this study.

Balance on an Account

As time passes by, a ledger account may accumulate several items on both the debit and credit sides. It is useful, as will be seen later, to know the net effect of all these entries, that is, to total the debit and credit items and ascertain the difference between the two. This difference is called the *balance* on the account; if the debit items exceed the credit items in value it is termed a *debit balance* and conversely if the credit items exceed the debit items the result is a *credit balance*.

The book-keeping routine for balancing an account may be demonstrated as follows:

BANK A/c

	£		£
Goods sold	100	Wages paid	20
		J. Smith paid	40
		Balance c/d	40
	£100		£100
Balance b/d	40		

Note the tidy way in which the account is made to balance by inserting the balance and then repeating the figure below the line. Note also the use of the abbreviations c/d (carried down) and b/d (brought down, i.e. brought down below the line from above). In this example there is thus a debit balance of £40 on the bank A/c, indicating that debits (items coming into the bank) exceed credits (items going out of the bank) by £40, or in other words there is a £40 balance in hand at the bank.

The general significance of balances on various classes of account may be summarized as follows:

Accounts classificiation	Debit balance signifies	Credit balance signifies
Personal A/cs	Amount owing to the business (debtor)	Amount owing by the business (creditor)
Nominal A/cs	Accumulated expenses	Accumulated income
Real A/cs	Things owned by the business (e.g. cash, car), termed *assets*	Other amounts owing by the business, termed *liabilities*

Referring back to the example on page 12; before Transaction 2 was effected there was a credit balance of £1000 on J. Jones A/c, signifying that the business owed £1000 to J. Jones, who was thus a creditor; when Transaction 2 is effected, J. Jones A/c is said to be cleared and this is indicated by ruling a line under the figures on each side of the account.

Students often find difficulty in reconciling in their minds the fact that a debit balance on the bank A/c signifies a balance in hand at the bank with the fact that their personal bank statement shows a credit balance when there is a balance in hand! A few moments' thought will clear up the problem if it is remembered that the bank statement is a copy of the customer's personal A/c in the bank's ledger: thus this credit balance signifies an amount owing by the bank to the customer, i.e. a balance in hand from the customer's point of view.

Balancing the Books

If the principle of double entry has been faithfully followed, it automatically follows that at any time the total debits in the ledger should equal the total credits. Pursuing the argument a stage further, it also follows that the total debit balances should equal the total credit balances: if they do not, an error in book-keeping has been made. Double entry book-keeping thus provides its own built-in check on the arithmetical accuracy of the system by the preparation of a *Trial Balance*.

A trial balance is simply a list of all the balances in the ledger at any given date with debit balances put in one column and credit balances in an adjacent column. If the totals of the debit and credit balances agree, the books are said to balance. Note, however, that this is merely a proof of the arithmetical accuracy of entries which have been made—an entry may have been missed out altogether or put in the wrong account: this will not affect the arithmetical accuracy and will not therefore be revealed by the trial balance. These errors should come to light by imposing other checks on the book-keeping.

The mechanics of book-keeping have now been performed, an accurate record in money terms has been made of all business transactions and the books balance. The stage is now set to use this information to compile the two basic pieces of information vital to effective management of any business;

1. The profit earned over a period of time.
2. The financial position, or state of affairs, at a given date.

Quill Pen Book-keeping?

The description of traditional book-keeping above was very basic and did tend to reflect tedious manual transcription on hard copy records: this was simply to explain the basic principles. In practice it is not always a "quill pen" task: there is a wide spectrum of mechanical and electronic aids which eliminate this drudgery. There are several proprietary "one write" systems which eliminate the need for repetitive transcription; there are software packages to fit microcomputers; there are computer mainframe programmes. Moreover many such systems are designed to produce analyses and control information automatically as an additional bonus. But all systems reflect the basic principles described above. Data processing will be reviewed briefly in Chapter 18.

CHAPTER 3

Ascertainment of Profit or Loss and Financial Position

IF A trader buys ten articles for £100 and sells them for £150 a profit of £50 has been made on the deal. However, in order to acquire and sell these articles, the trader may have incurred other expenses (e.g. transport, wages, rent) of £30 which must be met and therefore the final profit is only £20. In accounting terminology, the £50 is referred to as *Gross Profit* (the difference between selling price and cost of goods sold) and the £20 is referred to as *Net Profit* (final profit, net of all expenses).

Cost of Goods Sold

One vital rule in preparation and interpretation of accounts is that like must be compared with like. In the above example, if the trader had started on 1st January with three articles valued at £10 each and ended up on 30th June with five articles valued at £10 each, still having purchased ten for £100 and with a sales income of £150, what would have been the gross profit?

Gross profit is *not* a comparison of sales with purchases but a comparison of sales with cost of goods sold. In this example the cost of goods sold was £80 as follows:

	Articles	Cost
		£
Opening stock on hand	3	30
Add purchases	10	100
	13	130
Less closing stock on hand	5	50
Goods sold are therefore	8	£80

The figure for sales was £150, therefore gross profit is £150 minus £80: or £70.

17

Relevance of Income and Expenditure

The rule of comparing like with like is extended to the computation of net profit. Net profit is computed for a period of time and must be the difference between all income and expenditure relevant to that period, irrespective of whether or not cash has been received for all the income or cash paid for all the expenditure.

Returning to the example of our trader, let us assume the £30 expenses is the result of spending cash during the period 1st January to 30th June as follows:

	£	
Transport	5	both relevant to period 1st January to 30th June
Wages	10	
Rent	12	for 12 months, 1st January to 31st December
Electricity	3	for 3 months, 1st January to 31st March (£2 owing for 3 months 1st April to 30th June)
	£30	

Although the transport and wages are relevant to the period under review, the rent paid relates to a period of 12 months whilst the electricity relates to part only of the period under review. It would therefore be misleading to charge the whole of the rent against the gross profit: £6 is the equitable, or relevant charge. Similarly £3 plus £2, or £5, is the equitable, or relevant charge for electricity.

On this basis, whilst £30 was actually spent in cash in the period, the actual expenditure incurred and relevant to the period under review is as follows:

	£	
Transport	5	
Wages	10	
Rent	6	1st January to 30th June only
Electricity	5	full charge 1st January to 30th June
	£26	

The true net profit earned in the period 1st January to 30th June is thus:

	£
Gross profit as above	70
Less expenditure incurred as above	26
Net profit earned	£44

Profit and Loss Account

This is the accounting document which is prepared to reveal the profit earned over a period of time, alternative names being Trading and Profit and Loss Account, Income Statement, Earnings Statement and Revenue Account. Note that it is an account and therefore in traditional format follows the layout of a ledger account. It is divided into two halves: the top half or Trading Section compares sales with cost of goods sold and reveals gross profit; the bottom half or Profit and Loss Section takes the gross profit from the trading section, sets against this the expenditure incurred and reveals the net profit. Such an account prepared from the information developed in the case of our trader would appear in the form displayed below.

OUR TRADER

PROFIT AND LOSS ACCOUNT
FOR THE PERIOD 1ST JANUARY TO 30TH JUNE

	£		£
Opening stock	30	Sales	150
Purchases	100	Closing stock	50
Gross profit carried to Profit and Loss section	70		
	£200		£200
Transport	5	Gross profit from trading section	70
Wages	10		
Rent	6		
Electricity	5		
Net profit	44		
	£70		£70

Note that the closing stock may appear on the credit side of the trading section. This gives the same effect as deducting it from opening stock plus purchases in arriving at cost of goods sold.

Departing from the traditional format however, the profit and loss account is frequently presented in vertical form as below:

PROFIT AND LOSS ACCOUNT
FOR THE PERIOD 1ST JANUARY TO 30TH JUNE

	£	£
Sales		150
Cost of goods sold:		
Opening stock	30	
Add purchases	100	
	130	
Less closing stock	50	80
Gross profit		70
Less other expenses:		
Transport	5	
Wages	10	
Rent	6	
Electricity	5	26
Net profit		£ 44

A profit and loss account is prepared, in practice, by transferring to this account all the balances on the nominal A/cs (income and expenditure) in the ledger (see chart of classification of accounts on page 13 and table of significance of balances on page 15). This is done at the end of the period under review, after making the adjustments for relevance demonstrated above.

Capital Account

On setting up in business a trader introduces capital which is credited to an account called the *capital account*. The credit balance on this account represents the amount owing by the business to the owner of that business and will at all times be represented by assets employed in the business, known as the *net worth* of the business.

Suppose a trader sets up in business with £1500 in cash, the book-keeping entry will be:

Dr Cash A/c	£1500	(value coming in)
Cr Capital A/c	£1500	(value going out from the owner)

and at this stage the owner's capital employed in the business is £1500, represented by cash £1500.

If the trader now buys a car for £1000 cash, the entry will be as on page 12, and although the owner's capital employed is still £1500, it is now represented by cash £500 and car £1000.

Any new capital which is introduced by the owner from time to time will be credited to the capital A/c; conversely any capital withdrawn from the business will be debited to (i.e. deducted from) the capital A/c.

Profit Belongs to the Owner

Quite obviously the profit earned over a period, after all charges have been met, belongs to the owner of the business and therefore the net profit is transferred to the capital account when the profit and loss account has been prepared. The reader may have wondered where was the credit off-setting the debit of £44 net profit in the form on page 19. The credit is in the capital account, representing the increase in owner's capital employed accruing from profit earned. Similarly a net loss would be debited to (deducted from) the capital account.

Balance Sheet

After completing the profit and loss account, the remaining balances appearing in the ledger are summarized in a statement called the *balance sheet*, from which can be ascertained the financial position of the business.

The chart appearing on page 13 will now be expanded to demonstrate the preparation of profit and loss account and balance sheet:

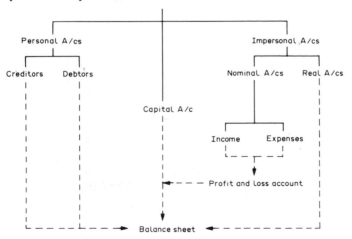

In traditional format, the balance sheet is a two-sided statement (it is not an account) listing liabilities or credit balances on the left and assets or debit balances on the right. This is the accepted manner of presentation in the U.K.—in America the sides are reversed. The section headed "Balancing the Books" on page 15 will explain also why the balance sheet balances: i.e. why the totals on the left- and right-hand sides agree.

Preparation of Balance Sheet

A balance sheet may be prepared any time one wishes to ascertain the financial position of the business and, in theory, one could be prepared after each book-keeping entry has been made. When the trader on page 20 set up in business the balance sheet would appear as follows:

Balance Sheet as at Transaction No. 1

Capital	£1500	Cash	£1500

Another balance sheet, prepared after buying the car, would appear as follows:

Balance Sheet as at Transaction No. 2

	£		£
Capital	1500	Cash	500
		Car	1000
	£1500		£1500

Suppose that the trader now buys stock for resale on credit for £200 and also buys a building for £1000, paying £100 cash and obtaining a mortgage for £900: these transactions would be reflected in the balance sheet as follows:

Balance Sheet as at Transactions Nos. 3 and 4

	£		£
Capital	1500	Cash	400
Mortgage	900	Car	1000
Creditor	200	Building	1000
		Stock	200
	£2600		£2600

Note that the owner's capital employed is still £1500. If the trader now sells stock costing £100 for £150 and incurs no other expense, the resulting profit of £50 will be added to the capital employed. If this sale is on credit, the resulting balance sheet will be:

Balance Sheet as at Transaction No. 5

	£		£
Capital	1500	Cash	400
Add profit	50	Car	1000
	——	Building	1000
	1550	Stock	100
Mortgage	900	Debtor	150
Creditor	200		
	——		——
	£2650		£2650

Balance Sheet Groupings

To assist in the interpretation of a balance sheet, the items are not strung out in a line as in the above example but are classified in major groups.

The assets (right-hand side) fall into two groups:

1. *Fixed assets* which are held permanently in the business, not for resale and without which the business could not be carried on. Examples are: land and buildings, plant and machinery, fixtures and fittings, motor vehicles.

2. *Current assets* which are held for conversion into cash at an early date in the normal course of business. Examples are: stock and work in progress, debtors, bank, cash. Sometimes these are called *circulating assets* because the items are continually changing their form in the normal course of business: thus stock is sold and becomes a debtor, the debtor pays and becomes cash, cash is used to buy more stock and so on, forever circulating.

The liabilities (left-hand side) fall into three main groups:

1. *Owner's capital employed.*

2. *Long-term liabilities* which are repayable after more than one year hence, e.g. a mortgage.

3. *Current liabilities* which are repayable within one year and in the normal course of business.

It is considered good practice to use these groupings and also, in the U.K., to list items in descending order of permanence, i.e. on the right-hand side: land at the top and cash at the bottom; on the left-hand side: the capital at the top and current liabilities at the bottom. In the balance sheet of a bank, where liquidity is important, the rule is broken and cash appears at the top of the right-hand side, but this is an exceptional type of business. In America, the reverse order is frequently used for all balance sheets.

It is not the nature of an asset which determines whether it is fixed or current but the manner in which it is employed in the business: a motor car used as a business vehicle is a fixed asset but a motor car held for resale by a motor dealer would in fact be stock, and therefore a current asset.

By adopting these groupings, the balance sheet appearing on page 23 is redrafted as follows:

Balance Sheet as at Transaction No. 5

	£		£	£
Owner's capital employed		*Fixed assets*		
Original capital	1500	Building	1000	
Add profit	50	Car	1000	
	———		———	2000
	1550	*Current assets*		
Long-term liabilities		Stock	100	
Mortgage	900	Trade debtors	150	
Current liabilities		Cash	400	
Trade creditors	200		———	650
	———			———
	£2650			£2650

Departing from traditional format, the balance sheet is frequently presented in vertical form as opposite.

The sub-totals revealed by this form of presentation are helpful in the interpretation of a balance sheet as we shall see later.

Fundamental Observations on the Balance Sheet

At this early stage it is important to observe these fundamental facts:

1. The balance sheet is not an account but is a statement of balances.

2. It is prepared at one point in time and is valid for that point in time only: the very next transaction of the business will render it out of date. A balance sheet artificially freezes the business for one split second in flight in the same way that a "still" from a film freezes the film for one split second.

Balance Sheet as at Transaction No. 5

	£	£
Fixed assets		
Building	1000	
Car	1000	
		2000
Current assets		
Stock	100	
Trade debtors	150	
Cash	400	
	650	
Deduct current liabilities		
Trade creditors	200	
Net current assets		450
Net assets		2450
Deduct amount financed by long-term liabilities		
Mortgage		900
Net worth		£1550
Represented by:		
Owner's capital employed		
Original capital		1500
Add profit		50
		£1550

3. It is designed simply to show whence the money has come to run the business—sources of funds (shown on the left-hand side of a traditional balance sheet) and how this money has been employed within the business—uses of funds (shown on the right-hand side of a traditional balance sheet).

4. Owner's capital employed is represented by the net worth of the business, i.e. total assets minus external liabilities. This can be demonstrated by reference to the redrafted balance sheet above, where owner's capital employed of £1550 = net worth of: £2000 + £650—£200—£900.

5. When profit has been earned it is not necessarily represented by cash in the till. In the above example a profit of £50 was made and yet cash went down from £1500 to £400 by the end of Transaction No. 5. Profit forms part of the owner's capital employed and therefore can be represented anywhere in the generality of net worth as explained under 4 above.

Relationship of Balance Sheet with Profit and Loss Account

The balance sheet and profit and loss account are interrelated documents. A balance sheet portrays the financial position at a certain date whilst the profit and loss account gives the detail behind one item in the balance sheet—the movement on owner's capital employed caused by profit or loss. In fact the net profit for a period can be computed without a profit and loss account by preparing a balance sheet at two dates. Any increase in net worth (i.e. owner's capital employed) between the two dates, after adjusting for capital introduced or withdrawn, must represent net profit earned in the period. Conversely a reduction in net worth represents net loss. In computing profit in this way there is a significant lack of detail which is provided by the profit and loss account. The balance sheet gives the final result, like the result of a football match in the stop press—the profit and loss account is the full report on the match, showing how that result came about.

There is a further link between balance sheet and profit and loss account. Earlier in this chapter was discussed the importance of adjusting actual cash receipts and payments to an incurred basis; in preparing the profit and loss account on page 19 the following adjustments were made:

1. £50 closing stock, in effect deducted from payment for purchases to arrive at cost of goods sold.

2. £6 rent in advance, or prepaid, deducted from payment for rent.

3. £2 electricity accrued due, added to payment for electricity.

These three adjustments are one half of a double entry; the other half features in the balance sheet as follows:

1. £50 closing stock appears as the first item in current assets.

2. £6 rent prepaid (this is a debit balance representing the theoretical right to a refund) also appears in current assets as *prepaid expenses* immediately following trade debtors.

3. £2 electricity accrued due (this is a credit balance representing a liability) appears in current liabilities as *accrued liabilities* immediately following trade creditors.

Accounting Period

A profit and loss account is prepared for and reveals the profit or loss of an accounting period. A balance sheet is prepared as at the end of the accounting period and reveals the financial position of the business as at that date.

The accounting period chosen is commonly a calendar year, hence the expression "Annual Accounts": meaning the profit and loss account and balance sheet for that year. However, whilst it is necessary to know the financial position at least once a year for tax and other legal matters, it is often desirable to know it at much more frequent intervals. Therefore an accounting period of 3 months' duration may be selected: indeed many businesses adopt a one month or a 4-week accounting period for internal reporting purposes.

At this stage the reader is again referred to the section "Time is an artificial compartment", on page 7. The relevance of this section may now be clearer.

The interrelationship of profit and loss account, balance sheet and accounting period may be summarized diagrammatically below, assuming a 12-month accounting period coinciding with the calendar year. The horizontal line represents a portion of time extracted from the continuing life of the business.

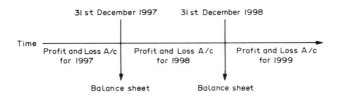

CHAPTER 4

Accounting Concepts, Bases of Valuation and Accounting Standards

TO RECAPITULATE on earlier chapters: when cash is spent the cash book (cash A/c) is credited, representing value going out of this account, and some other account is debited. If a nominal account is debited, a charge will ultimately be made to the profit and loss account; if a real account is debited, the amount will not be charged to the profit and loss account but will feature in the balance sheet as an asset. Does this create scope for manipulating profit up or down? Quite frankly both here and elsewhere there is considerable potential for manipulation of profit ("cosmetic accounting") and it is for this reason that we must digress at this stage and consider the basic accounting principles upon which profit is calculated and the need for standard accounting practices.

What is Profit?

£1 profit is not a real thing like a £1 coin, it is not cash but is an accounting concept based upon the application of accepted accounting rules (confirm this by rereading note 5 on page 25).

Similarly the totals at the foot of a balance sheet do not value *the business* (they may not even value *the assets* of the business in real terms) because these totals are also based upon application of the same accounting rules called concepts and conventions.

Accounting Concepts

There are many long-established rules or principles upon which the accounting concepts of profit and balance sheet valuation are based but the most important ones are as follows:

1. *The Going-concern Concept*

In putting together a profit and loss account and balance sheet the accountant presumes that the business is going to continue and not terminate at the balance sheet date. Therefore the accountant is not concerned with break-up values but with continuing values in use to a going concern. We shall see below how the application of this concept affects the valuation of the assets which appear in the balance sheet.

2. *The Concept of Relevance*

In putting a profit and loss account together the accountant is concerned, not with cash receipts and cash payments, but with those items of income and expenditure deemed to be relevant to the period under review. Sometimes referred to as the "matching principle" or "accrual accounting" the application of this concept was well demonstrated in the first two sections of the previous chapter ("Cost of Goods Sold" and "Relevance of Income and Expenditure") on pages 17 and 18.

3. *The Concept of Prudence*

The accountant is trained to be prudent, or conservative, in putting together a profit and loss account and balance sheet. Whenever there is doubt it will be resolved in the least favourable light, always anticipating any potential losses but ignoring profits which *might* not materialize. We shall see below how this "belt and braces" concept affects the valuation of current assets in the balance sheet.

4. *Consistency*

Once the accountant has determined how the principles or concepts of accounting (including the three mentioned above) will be applied, they will typically continue to be applied in the same way year after year. The application of the concept of consistency therefore renders trend and other comparisons much more reliable: as was stated on page 17 "one vital rule in preparation and interpretation of accounts is that like must be compared with like."

Later sections of this chapter lead us gently into some of the areas where the application of accounting concepts is most significant.

Accounting Conventions

Over and above the concepts of accounting there are also two basic conventions of accounting:

1. The Historical Cost Convention

This is the oldest of the two and implies that figures in the profit and loss account and balance sheet normally ignore the impact of inflation. Such figures normally reflect costs or values which were current historically when the original entry was made in the books. Accounting is seldom "pure" and even under the historical cost convention some firms have chosen periodically to revalue fixed assets in the balance sheet—but this still does not necessarily reflect current costs or present-day values once the revaluation date becomes history.

2. The Current Cost Convention

Still relatively new, and therefore somewhat contentious, this convention implies that some or all of the figures in the profit and loss account and balance sheet will take account of inflation and so reflect current costs and present-day values at each balance sheet date. The subject of Current Cost Accounting is taken up in a later chapter.

Capital and Revenue Expenditure

Capital expenditure is that which results in the acquisition of a permanent or long-lasting asset or which extends or enhances the earning capacity of the existing assets of the business. This type of expenditure will be debited to a real account and will feature as a fixed asset in the balance sheet.

Revenue expenditure represents the normal day-to-day running expenses of the business and does not result in the acquisition of a fixed asset. Expenditure incurred in maintaining the fixed assets in efficient working order; costs of manufacture, selling and distribution; expenses of administration and management are all examples of revenue expenditure. This type of expenditure will be debited to a nominal account and will thus be a charge to the profit and loss account.

Note that it is not the nature of the expenditure but the purpose for which it is incurred which determines whether it is capital or revenue expenditure. Thus wages paid to an employee will normally be revenue expenditure, i.e.

a normal running expense; however, if that employee were engaged on, say, installing a brand-new central heating system to the factory, his wages will be capital expenditure.

The reader will notice a similarity here to the rules of distinction between fixed and current assets; again it is the purpose for which expenditure is incurred, not the nature of the expenditure, which determines its definition.

Revenue expenditure is written off, i.e. charged, or debited, to profit and loss account during the year in which it is incurred. The concept of relevance is applied in determining the amount to write off: this was demonstrated in the first two sections of the previous chapter. The concept of relevance is now carried a stage further and applied to capital expenditure. This is expenditure relevant to a number of years—in fact the years during which the asset thereby acquired will provide a useful service to the business. Capital expenditure is therefore written off to profit and loss account over the useful working life of the fixed asset thereby acquired, the amount written off being termed depreciation.

Depreciation of Fixed Assets

The object of charging depreciation arises from the concept of relevance and was introduced above but it bears repetition: it is *to write off to profit and loss account the cost of a fixed asset over its useful working life.* Many misconceptions in accounts interpretation arise when this simple fact is overlooked. In particular, the following points arise:

1. Under the historical cost convention,

(a) The value at which a fixed asset appears in the balance sheet is original cost (or occasionally, in the case of freehold land and buildings, a periodic revaluation) less accumulated depreciation to date—note that this does not represent a current purchase or resale price.

(b) Fluctuations in market value taking place after initial purchase of an asset are ignored by the balance sheet as these have no bearing upon the concept of depreciation. Furthermore, fixed assets are not held for resale in the normal course of business and so the going concern concept dictates that market value is of no consequence.

2. Under the current cost convention, however, the value of a fixed asset is net current replacement cost: i.e. estimated replacement cost scaled down by the proportion of its life expired.

3. The fact that a fixed asset becomes obsolete is ignored when calculating depreciation as such, although application of the concept of prudence might suggest an additional deduction from profits for obsolescence if the firm now decides to reassess the asset's useful working life. However, if the obsolescence is realized (as when it is deemed prudent to sell an obsolete item and replace) it represents a loss on disposal and will be taken into account as such—but this is not depreciation.

Methods of Depreciation

If the object of depreciation is as stated above, it follows that the logical method of computing an annual charge for depreciation is to apply the formula:

$$\frac{\text{original cost* minus estimated residual (scrap or resale) value}}{\text{estimated number of years useful life}}$$

This will obviously produce an equal annual charge and if it were plotted on a graph a straight line would result. Hence this method is referred to as the *straight line* or *fixed instalment* method of depreciation.

A big practical problem is to estimate the number of years' useful life—who will be bold enough to estimate this? If the firm has a definite replacement policy based on a term of years or if the asset has a known life span, as with a lease for a stated number of years, the estimate is simple: in all other cases it is not so simple. For this reason, the historical cost convention permits an alternative to the straight line method and the *reducing balance* method is commonly used. By this method a fixed percentage is applied to the reducing balance of the asset each year, for example:

		£
Original cost of asset		1000
Depreciation year 1:	10%	100
Balance sheet value at end of year 1		900
Depreciation year 2:	10% of £900	90
Balance sheet value at end of year 2		810
Depreciation year 3:	10% of £810	81 and so on

* Or estimated replacement cost, if the current cost convention is used.

Compare this with the straight line method and notice in particular that the depreciation charge reduces annually and that the balance sheet value can never be eliminated under this method.

A variation on the straight line method is the depletion unit method which is applied to wasting assets such as mines or quarries. Asset life is estimated in units of output instead of years and a rate of depreciation is computed per unit of output, e.g. per tonne of saleable ore raised. Depreciation to be written off in any year is ascertained by multiplying the actual units of output for that year by the unit rate of depreciation. As with the normal straight line method, the object is to depreciate the asset fully by the time it is worked out.

In the case of assets with a doubtful life and of comparatively small value (e.g. loose tools or livestock) the *valuation* method is used whereby the asset is valued each year, the difference between valuation and book value being deemed to be the depreciation charge for the year.

The method of depreciation to be selected will be the one most suited to the particular fixed asset being depreciated and, once selected, the consistency concept determines that it should be applied consistently each year. There are other more sophisticated methods of depreciation in use, but those outlined in this section are the ones commonly employed in practice.

Valuation of Current Assets

The two accounting concepts of going concern and prudence help to determine the basis of valuation of current assets. Unlike fixed assets, it will be remembered that current assets *are* held for conversion into cash at at an early date, and therefore, for balance sheet purposes, a basis of valuation is used which is quite different from that outlined above for fixed assets. A current asset should not appear in the balance sheet at a value in excess of its estimated realizable value on conversion into cash and, therefore, the basis adopted is "the *lower* of cost or realizable value" (under the historical cost convention) or "the *lower* of replacement value or realizable value" (under the current cost convention). Here we see the accounting concept of prudence hard at work because this basis of valuation writes off any anticipated or suspected loss but ignores any profit until it is actually realized.

Rules are not always easy to apply and that relating to the balance-sheet valuation of stock is no exception. Refer back to the calculation of goods sold on page 17: it was not difficult to value those five remaining articles at the lower of cost or realizable value; it had to be £10. But take the following example:

My purchases in a period were—

Articles	Cost each	Total cost
	£	£
10	10	100
10	15	150
10	20	200
30		£450

and at the end of the period I have left in stock five articles with a realizable value of £30 each. Clearly for balance-sheet purposes they must be valued at cost because this is the lower ... but what is their cost? There are at least three answers:

1. The FIFO basis of valuation (First In First Out) implies that the five in stock must be part of the final delivery and therefore would be valued at £20 each.

2. On the other hand, LIFO (Last In First Out) would imply that they were part of the initial delivery and therefore would be valued at £10 each.

3. Whilst the average method would clearly value them at £15 each!

Referring back to page 17, you will notice that the value of closing stock is deducted from purchases to arrive at the cost of goods sold. Therefore the valuation of stock must also affect profit as demonstrated below:

	FIFO	LIFO	Average
	£	£	£
Cost of 30 articles purchased	450	450	450
Less closing stock on hand			
(5 articles)	100	50	75
Cost of goods sold (25 articles)	350	400	375
If sold for £30 each	750	750	750
Profit	£400	£350	£375

Notice that the higher is the figure for stock, the higher is the resultant profit, and vice versa.

Rather like the selection of a method of depreciation so with the selection of a method of stock valuation, the consistency concept determines that, once selected, it should be applied consistently each year.

Goodwill

What is a business worth? Sufficient should have been said in this chapter to make the reader realize that the balance sheet valuation of assets is no reliable guide to the "true value" (in non-accounting terminology) of a business. Except on a forced sale, current assets should not be worth less than their balance sheet value—although of course they may be worth more. Fixed assets may be worth more or less than their balance sheet value, depending upon the interplay of the forces of obsolescence, changing money values and market trends. An up-to-date value may of course be obtained by professional valuation of both fixed and current assets but this is a value of the business assets only, not of the *business*.

The true value of any commodity is whatever a willing buyer is prepared to pay.

A business may be worth much more than the value of its tangible assets due to valuable business contacts, market outlets, production facilities, geographical location, reputation of business, brand names, exclusive or monopoly rights, site development potential to mention but a few. How much are you willing to pay for this business—how badly do you want it? The amount you are willing to pay for these intangible attributes is termed *goodwill*.

Consider the following balance sheet of a business:

	£		£
Capital	1000	Fixed assets	800
		Current assets	200
	£1000		£1000

For reasons known only to myself I am willing to pay £1500 for this business compared to the balance sheet value of its assets of £1000: I am therefore paying £500 for goodwill. Having raised capital of £1500 with which to purchase the business, my opening balance sheet will appear as follows:

	£		£
Capital	1500	Purchased goodwill	500
		Fixed assets	800
		Current assets	200
	£1500		£1500

The fact that purchased goodwill now appears amongst the assets in my balance sheet does not invest the balance sheet with any greater ability to reflect a true commercial value of the business. Goodwill itself may be valuable one day and worthless the next depending upon the presence or absence of a willing buyer or buyers.

Goodwill may be quite substantial in relation to other more tangible assets, on the other hand it may be of negative value. Consider two extreme cases:

1. A milk round with no tangible assets at all yet which sells for £1500—100 percent goodwill.

2. A gold mine with a shaft sunk and equipment valued at £150,000 but unfortunately no gold is found—the value of a hole in the ground with nothing at the bottom perhaps depends on an alternate use, say as a rubbish tip.

So *should* purchased goodwill appear amongst the assets in the balance sheet if the true value is ephemeral? At the time of writing, the standard accounting treatment in North America *is* to show purchased goodwill as a fixed asset and then to depreciate it in a similar manner to other fixed assets; but the most frequent accounting treatment in the U.K. is *not* to show purchased goodwill as an asset but instead to deduct it from reserves (i.e. the accumulation of profits retained) in the balance sheet: this is demonstrated in the John Waddington published accounts at page 226, note 17 and explained in the accounting policies at page 216.

Valuation of Goodwill

How did I arrive at the price of £1500 for the above business, thereby valuing goodwill at £500? Many academic, and sometimes questionable, methods of "valuing" goodwill have been proposed, and indeed used, from time to time. Perhaps the method with most to recommend it, and which will be discussed below, is that of capitalizing future maintainable profits.

All other things being equal, the more potentially profitable a business is, the more valuable will it be. Goodwill is thus indirectly related to profit because goodwill becomes more valuable as the potential profit from the balance sheet value of a business increases. A genuine purchaser asks himself two questions when valuing a business: what profit am I going to get from this business in future, under my management?; what rate of return do I want on my investment?

Assuming that the business under consideration has estimated future maintainable profits of £300 per annum and that I require a return of 20 percent per annum on my investment, the most I am willing to pay for this business is:

$$\frac{100}{20} \times £300 \text{ or } £1500$$

Estimated future maintainable profits have been *capitalized* by this calculation to £1500, i.e. they represent an annual return at the desired percentage (20 percent) of this figure. Had I required a return of only 10 percent on my investment, I would similarly have been prepared to pay £3000 for the business.

This method of valuing a business, and thereby goodwill, assumes a "genuine" purchaser who requires the business for normal trading purposes. On the other hand, the purchaser may realize that there is undeveloped site potential and in this case he will value the business at whatever figure is acceptable to the seller, provided that it leaves the purchaser a satisfactory margin for a quick capital profit on resale or development. Estimated maintainable future profits are ignored because the purchaser has no intention of perpetuating the business.

There can be no one simple formula for valuing goodwill because it is so much a personal matter between the seller and an individual willing buyer. To repeat from page 35: "How much are you willing to pay for this business—how badly do you want it?"

Valuation of Brands

A matter not unrelated to the true value of a business, and hence to the value of goodwill, is the presence of valuable brand names. Therefore should the value of brands appear on the balance sheet and if so how should they be valued? And if so, should they be depreciated?

In the U.K., John Waddington is the owner of the brand "Monopoly" and other board games. Presumably these names have value in their own right, yet nothing appears in Waddington's balance sheet on page 213 for these items. On the other hand some companies, particularly in consumer goods, alcoholic beverages and newspapers, have computed quite significant values for their brands and incorporated these values into their balance sheets.

Remember that "the value" of purchased goodwill is the difference between the value paid for a business and the balance sheet value of assets thereby acquired. Presumably therefore, the amount "paid for" goodwill will be higher if the assets acquired do not include a figure for brands than if they do.

Valuation of Other "Intangible Assets"

In the same way that brands might represent considerable value to the business, other intangibles might also be of value: key employees for instance. Without doubt the value of, say, a consultancy or research business is heavily dependent on the existence of such key employees. So should a value be placed upon them for balance sheet purposes? (And should this value subsequently be depreciated?)

Whereas there is an academic body of knowledge referred to as "human asset accounting", it is not common practice at the time of writing to incorporate a value for human assets in the balance sheet.

Balance Sheet Story

A balance sheet can never tell us what a business is worth, because this simply is not the purpose of the balance sheet. What then can it tell us? The story told by a balance sheet can be most interesting and illuminating; we shall be taking a closer look at a balance sheet in Chapter 11. However, before then it is necessary to discourse upon other matters.

Scope for Opinion

Returning to the preamble to this chapter and to what has been said about the application of accounting concepts, conventions and bases of valuation, it must now be clear to the reader that there *is* certainly scope for opinion and therefore, unfortunately, scope for manipulation of profit and balance sheet values. The very words "going concern", "relevance", "prudence" and "consistency" are largely soft, subjective grey concepts rather than hard, objective, black and white facts. For this reason profit itself must be largely a soft, subjective, grey concept rather than the hard, objective fact of, say, a £ coin.

Two honest accountants faced with the same trial balance might express different opinions as to, for example: what is capital and what is revenue; how to depreciate fixed assets; how to value stock—and thereby produce quite different profits and balance sheet valuations. I repeat, two honest accountants might do this: how much more therefore might an unscrupulous one do? Whether it was deliberately unscrupulous or whether it was simply a matter of opinion is academic but a number of celebrated cases (e.g. Rolls Royce who, before changing their policy on this matter, increased reported profits by some £20 million by classifying research and development expenditure as capital rather than revenue expenditure; GEC who saw a takeover profit forecast of £10 million by AEI turn into a loss of £4½ million on a change in basis of stock valuation) brought bad odour upon the accounting profession who therefore felt that perhaps the time had come to constrain the scope for opinion or at least have it brought out into the open. And so, Accounting Standards were born.

Accounting Standards

Late in 1969 the Council of the Institute of Chartered Accountants in England and Wales first set in motion the procedure to narrow the scope for opinion, the areas of difference and the variety in accounting practice by publishing authoritative Statements of Standard Accounting Practice (SSAPs) on contentious items. What was to become the Accounting Standards Committee was formed, its membership eventually embracing all the major professional accounting Institutes and accounts users (e.g. brokers).

The procedure was for the Accounting Standards Committee (ASC) to publish an Exposure Draft (ED) as a discussion document and to allow a period for interested parties to submit their views before the final SSAP was published. The ASC was disbanded in 1990, by which time the following SSAPs were in force:

SSAP		Effective from
1	Accounting for associated	Jan. 1971
	companies	(revised May 1982)
2	Disclosure of accounting policies	Jan. 1972
3	Earnings per share	Jan. 1972
		(revised Aug. 1974)
4	Accounting for government grants	Jan. 1974
		(revised July 1990)
5	Accounting for value-added tax	Jan. 1974
6	Extraordinary items and prior year adjustments	Jan. 1974
		(revised July 1986)
8	Treatment of taxation under the imputation	Jan. 1975
	system in the accounts of companies	(revised Jan. 1978)

9	Stocks and long term contracts	Jan. 1976
		(revised Sept. 1988)
10	Statements of Source and Application of Funds	Jan. 1976
12	Accounting for depreciation	Jan. 1978
		(revised Jan. 1987)
13	Accounting for research and development	Jan. 1978
		(revised Jan. 1989)
14	Group accounts	Jan. 1979
15	Accounting for deferred tax	Jan. 1979
		(revised Apr. 1985)
17	Accounting for post balance sheet events	Sept. 1980
18	Accounting for contingencies	Sept. 1980
19	Accounting for investment properties	July. 1981
20	Foreign currency translation	Apr. 1983
21	Accounting for leases and hire purchase contracts	July 1984
22	Accounting for goodwill	Jan. 1985
		(revised July 1989)
23	Accounting for acquisitions and mergers	Apr. 1985
24	Accounting for pension costs	July 1988
25	Segmental reporting	July 1990

In February 1990, in an attempt to give more weight and authority to the accounting standard setting process and to act as a powerful proactive public influence for ensuring good accounting practice, the U.K. Government announced the establishment of the Financial Reporting Council (FRC) covering, at a high level, a wide constituency of interests. Its chairman is appointed jointly by the Secretary of State for Industry and the Governor of the Bank of England; the first chairman was Sir Ron Dearing. The FRC oversees the work of two further bodies: the Accounting Standards Board (ASB) and the Financial Reporting Review Panel. The Panel's responsibility is to enquire into cases where it appears that the requirements of the Companies Acts or Accounting Standards might have been breached.

The ASB is a much stronger body than the ASC which it replaces. Its total membership is nine including a full-time chairman and technical director; it is financed by the accounting profession, the financial community and the Government. The ASB has endorsed all the SSAPs listed above and has started adding its own Financial Reporting Standards (FRSs) following the publication of exposure drafts (which, believe it or not, are called FREDs). The first FRSs are:

FRS		Effective from
1	Cash flow statements	Mar. 1992
2	Accounting for subsidiary undertakings	Dec. 1992
3	Reporting financial performance	Jan. 1993

Legal weight was given to accounting standards in the U.K. for the first time by the Companies Act 1989 with the requirement that directors of large companies disclose in their published accounts that the accounts have been prepared in accordance with applicable accounting standards, or to give their reasons for departure therefrom. In extreme cases the Court may order the preparation of revised accounts.

The U.K. is not the only country to publish accounting standards but is further down the road than some. However, for many years the U.S.A. has had its equivalent standard setting body: the Financial Accounting Standards Board or FASB. The EC is moving slowly but meanwhile there is an attempt to develop international accounting standards via the International Accounting Standards Board. It is ironic that we have moved relatively quickly from a free-for-all situation to one that some see as in danger of over-proliferation of standards. The path has not been easy; indeed some SSAPs took a very long time to progress from EDs, some SSAPs have been rethought and revised more than once, some EDs have never got off the starting line, whilst some SSAPs are not being followed by a minority for reasons best known to themselves. It seems that the accountant's time-honoured prerogative to express opinions dies hard!

Accounting Policies

Despite the existence of accounting standards there is still some scope for the expression of opinion by accountants, the consequence of which will be to compute and report different profit figures and different balance sheet values from the same raw data. Some occasions where this can occur, for example, are the computation of depreciation, the valuation of stocks and work in progress, the conversion of foreign currencies, the valuation and treatment of goodwill, to name but four.

In such circumstances, where more than one accounting basis is acceptable, the accounting policy adopted must be explained so that the reader can correctly interpret any financial information published by a business. Hence, SSAP 2 requires the publication of key accounting policies which will explain how contentious items have been dealt with in the accounts.

A representative example of the disclosure of accounting policies appears at page 216 for John Waddington PLC.

CHAPTER 5

The Limited Company

THE form of organization considered in Chapters 2 and 3 has been that of *sole trader*—one person managing their own business, using capital provided from their own savings or on trust from close friends or relations. Their personal capital and livelihood are, legally, indistinguishable from those of their business—although clearly there should be an accounting distinction!

Businesses grow and require more capital to finance this growth: friends are no longer willing or able to put up large amounts of capital on trust and, to safeguard their interests, those who do provide capital may look for a share in the management. A form of organization which provides this safeguard is a *partnership*, set up under the Partnership Act 1890, whereby two or more persons jointly share in the capital, profits or losses and management of the business. A partnership can become unwieldy when a large number of partners is taking an active part in management, even though the maximum number of partners is limited by law to twenty (except for accountants, solicitors and members of a recognized stock exchange). Furthermore, any partner can be called upon to meet *all* the partnership debts to the last penny of their private possessions,* irrespective of the amount of capital the partner has agreed to contribute, if the other partners default or otherwise fail to contribute their agreed capital: in other words, the *liability of a partner is unlimited*.

A partnership therefore may be far from a happy association and, if business is to grow freely, there is need for a form of organization whereby many persons can contribute varying amounts of capital, without necessarily taking an active part in management and with the knowledge that their total liability will be limited to a predetermined amount. The Limited Liability Company was created to fill this need.

---

* In actual fact, under the laws of bankruptcy, they would be allowed to retain their tools of trade and the necessary wearing apparel and bedding of themselves, spouse and children.

Legal Status

A limited company is formed under the Companies Acts 1985 and 1989 or under an earlier Act. The 1985 Act consolidated the early Acts of 1948, 1967, 1976, 1980 and 1981, the 1989 Act introduced further amendments.

At law, a limited company is an artificial person with its own legal rights and privileges quite distinct from those of the members who compose it. This is a vital distinction from the sole trader and partnership forms of organization considered above where there is no separate legal entity. It is this separation of legal rights which admits the principle of *limited liability* whereby a member (one legal person) contracts with the company (another legal person) to advance a certain limited amount of money as that member's share of the capital required by that company.

Memorandum and Articles of Association

The full legal formalities of forming a limited company are beyond the scope of this book, but two documents which must be filed with the Registrar of Companies are important and are considered in some detail—the "Memorandum" and "Articles".

Because a limited company has a separate legal status there must be some document which evidences its existence (we have a birth certificate or passport), so when a limited company is formed a *Memorandum of Association* is prepared. This is a formal document containing the following five clauses or sections:

1. The name of the company: "limited" or "p.l.c." (or the Welsh equivalent) must be the last word.

2. The country in which the registered office is situate: this is the company's nationality—necessary to determine which law shall apply.

3. The objects of the company: what was the company formed to do? This is a vital clause and must be drafted as widely as possible (it is not uncommon for this clause to run to several pages in length) because a limited company, by law, cannot perform any act not included in this Objects Clause. It is possible subsequently to alter a company's objects, but this can be a troublesome legal process.

4. A simple statement that the liability of members is limited.

5. The maximum amount of share capital and its division into shares of various classes; these terms are discussed later.

A limited company is similar to a club in that it is composed of members; therefore it is necessary to have a set of club rules, governing the internal running of the club and the rights and obligations of its members. The Memorandum, in recognizing the existence and purpose of a limited company, regulates the company's relationship with the outside world; there must be, therefore, another document akin to the club rules and this is the *Articles of Association*. The Articles comprise a formal document, sister to the Memorandum, and may be drafted especially for the company, or alternatively a model set of articles (Table A) is embraced in the Companies Act 1985 which may be adopted instead. Examples of the points covered by Table A are: issue of shares to members and payment thereof, conduct of meetings, appointment and duties of directors, distribution of profit.

The Memorandum and Articles of a limited company are among the documents which must be filed with the Registrar of Companies and which may be inspected by any member of the public on payment of a nominal search fee.

Public and Private Companies

There are three stages in transition from a partnership. Firstly a company may be formed to reap the benefits of limited liability but still continue in a small way with a few "family" members. Provided such a company has a minimum of two members and, by its Articles, prohibits the open invitation to the public to subscribe capital, it earns the title *Limited Company* or *Ltd*. i.e. a non public, or private company. A private company is exempt from certain of the formalities which would otherwise have to be complied with under the Companies Acts.

The second stage is reached when a private company wishes to expand its number of members and offer shares or debentures to the public and so becomes a *Public Limited Company* or *PLC*.

A further stage is reached when the company seeks an official quotation on a Stock Exchange and thence looks to the public at large to provide capital through the new issues machinery of the Stock Exchange. It is to protect this investing public that the Companies Acts contain many regulations and provisions concerning disclosure of a company's activities and financial position. These regulations as to disclosure get more severe as the size of the company gets bigger.

Share Capital

Membership of a company is obtained by subscribing towards the share capital, i.e. taking a share in the capital of the company. A share may be purchased direct from the company upon an initial issue or, in the case of a public company, on the Stock Exchange from a member wishing to dispose of part or all of his holding. As a result of Stock Exchange dealings members of a public company are a constantly changing body, but this does not affect the company itself in view of its separate legal status.

In considering share capital, certain terminology must be understood:

1. *Authorized share capital* is the maximum amount of capital a company is *authorized* to issue by the fifth clause of its Memorandum. When a company is formed, stamp duty is payable on this authorized amount and any subsequent increase similarly attracts additional stamp duty.

2. *Allotted*, or *Issued share capital* is that part of the authorized share capital which the company has actually issued to its members.

3. *Called up capital* is that part of the allotted share capital which the members have been called upon to pay. If a company requires capital to flow in over a period of time as required, rather than all at once, it will make "calls" on the members of so much per share until the full amount of the shares has been called.

4. *Paid up capital* is that part of the called up capital which has actually been paid in cash. Any difference between these two represents a call in arrear and if the member does not pay this amount within a reasonable time he is liable to have his shares forfeited under the terms of the articles of association. When the full value of the allotted capital has been called and paid up, it is said to be *fully paid.*

Classes of Share

A choice of investment prospects must be made available to suit the different tastes of the investing public: some require a guaranteed fixed income, others subordinate income to capital growth, some are willing to speculate both capital and income, whilst others look for security of capital at a consequently lower rate of income. Our Stock Exchange system provides a wide range of securities but individual companies also seek to attract different sections of the investing public by offering various classes of share, the two most common being preference and ordinary shares.

Preference Shares

The rights of these shares are set out in the Articles but normally they carry a fixed rate of dividend which has preference over the dividend on any other class of share when profits are being distributed to members. Payment of this fixed amount must be all or nothing at all and, if in any year there is insufficient profit to meet the full amount, the right to a dividend in that year is lost. However, with *cumulative preference shares*, any unpaid amounts may be carried forward without time limit and still have priority for payment out of future profits. A further attribute of a preference share is its preference over other classes of share for repayment of capital if the company is wound up (i.e. its existence terminated).

Normally, winding up is the only occasion when capital is returned to members, but a further type of preference share is a *redeemable preference share* which will be redeemed by the company: that is repayment will be made to members, within a stipulated time.

Yet another type of preference share is a *participating preference share*, which carries the right to a further share in profits in addition to their fixed dividend after ordinary shareholders have been paid a certain percentage dividend.

The full title of a preference share will indicate which type it is: a "6 per cent Cumulative Redeemable Preference Share 2000-5", for example, is a preference share which carries the right to a fixed annual dividend of 6 per cent of the nominal value of the share and, should there be insufficient profit in any year to meet this dividend, the right accumulates until paid in full; the share will be repaid sometime between 1st January 2000 and 31st December 2005.

Ordinary Shares

Alternatively known as *equity shares*, these shares carry no preferential rights but are entitled to the whole of the profits (but not necessarily as a dividend) and capital of the company after prior claims of preference shareholders have been met. The bulk of capital issued by most limited companies is of this type. Success or failure of an equity share depends upon the success or failure of the company itself: when profits are high, ordinary dividends will be high; when the value of capital employed in the business increases, the value of the ordinary share will increase—and of course vice versa.

The Companies Act 1981 permitted a company for the first time to buy back, or redeem, ordinary shares subject to compliance with certain formalities. Prior to that Act, such action was illegal.

Deferred or *founder's shares* are a type of ordinary share carrying the right to a dividend only after a certain percentage has been paid on ordinary shares. These shares are usually issued to vendors of a business in part settlement of purchase consideration. During negotiations for purchase of a business, the vendor will no doubt paint a glowing picture of future profit potential to support the asking price and so acceptance of a deferred share will add weight to such claims and serve as an earnest.

"A" and "B" shares are sometimes met in practice, indicating that there is some difference in the rights of the "A" and "B" shareholder, usually in the right to vote at general meetings of the company.

Debentures

A company may raise capital by means of a loan in addition to the issue of shares. A debenture is a document which acknowledges such a loan and stipulates the terms for repayment, the interest payable and the assets, if any, upon which the loan is secured. There are different types of debentures: a *fixed debenture* or *mortgage debenture* is secured upon a stipulated asset similar to a mortgage secured upon one's house; a *floating debenture* confers a general charge not attached to any specific asset; *unsecured loan notes* are an unsecured debenture issued by large well-known companies which carry the public's confidence to the point where no security need be offered for a loan.

Shares and debentures are both dealt in on the Stock Exchange and are often referred to as if they were the same thing. There is an important distinction between the two and the fundamental differences are summarized below:

Share	Debenture
1 A share is part of the capital	A debenture is a loan
2 A shareholder is a member or part owner of the company	A debenture holder is a creditor of the company
3 There is no security of capital	A debenture may be secured
4 A shareholder is remunerated by dividend which is a share of profits. If there are no profits there can be no dividend	A debenture holder is paid interest which must be met whether there are profits or not
5 A preference share has priority over an ordinary share both as to dividend and capital	A debenture has priority over both preference and ordinary shares both as to interest and repayment of capital
6 A share may or may not be repayable	A debenture *must* be repaid or assets will be seized to effect repayment

Board of Directors

Comparison was drawn earlier in this chapter between a limited company and a club, and this comparison can be repeated when considering the management structure: both forms of organization are run by a committee of members, some of whom may be salaried. In the case of a limited company this committee is known as the board of directors. Directors are elected by members in general meeting and the Articles normally provide for one-third of the board to retire annually by rotation, although retiring directors may stand for re-election. The board will elect one of their number to act as their chairman (who will thereby also be *chairman of the company*) and another, to take responsibility for day-to-day management of the company, who will be called the *managing director*.

Primarily, therefore, control of a company is exercised by the managing director, but he is responsible to the board, which is in turn responsible to the members. Ultimate control of a limited company is thus in the hands of members who have power, by their vote in general meeting, to remove the board or the managing director if they are dissatisfied with the board's conduct of the company's affairs. An important guide to the effectiveness of the board's conduct of the company's affairs is provided for the members in the annual published profit and loss account and balance sheet. These will be discussed in the next two chapters.

CHAPTER 6

Annual Accounts of a Limited Company

IN CHAPTER 3 we saw how a profit and loss account and balance sheet (collectively termed "annual accounts") are produced for a sole trader. Annual accounts of a limited company are prepared in exactly the same way up to the point where the net profit is ascertained. Attention was drawn in Chapter 3 to the fact that, because net profit belongs to the owner, it is added to his capital in the balance sheet. Whilst this is also true of a limited company, there are slight variations in principle due to there now being many joint owners (i.e. shareholders), each of whom looks for a share of profits (i.e. dividend) to remunerate their capital invested. These necessary variations in principle thus concern the treatment of profit and capital.

Treatment of Profit

Page 20 gave an example, in vertical form, of the profit and loss account for a sole trader. The format for a limited company is essentially similar but has a further section at the foot which shows how the net profit has been dealt with, or *appropriated*: hence this section is often referred to as the *appropriation section* (cf the trading section and profit and loss section referred to on page 19).

The following appropriations would normally be made:

interest payable on borrowed money,

corporation tax payable on taxable profits,

dividend payable to shareholders,

and the balance of profit which is unappropriated will be added to the shareholders' capital in the balance sheet just as the net profit was added to the sole trader's capital on page 25.

49

The Profit Family

To differentiate one member of a family from another, each one is given his or her own personal first name, e.g. Dorothy Hartley, Colin Hartley. Hartley is the family name; Dorothy and Colin are two specific members of the Hartley family. Similarly Profit is a family name and specific members of that family must be given their own personal first name.

Up until now we have considered only two members of the Profit family: Gross Profit and Net Profit. When reporting the profit of a limited company the family grows but the name Net Profit is not normally used because there could be some confusion as to exactly what it might be "net" of: net of interest? net of tax? net of dividend? or what? So the following six, more specifically named, members of the Profit family are frequently met in the profit and loss account of a limited company:

     Sales (sometimes called Turnover)
     deduct cost of goods sold
1   = GROSS PROFIT
     deduct other operating costs
2   = OPERATING PROFIT (sometimes called TRADING PROFIT)
     deduct interest payable on borrowed money plus
     any non-operating income (e.g. interest received)
3   = PROFIT BEFORE TAXATION
     deduct corporation tax payable on taxable profits
4   = PROFIT AFTER TAXATION (this is the profit which is now attributable to all shareholders)
     deduct profit, if any, attributable to other than ordinary shareholders, e.g.
       i. dividend payable to preference shareholders
       ii. profit attributable to minority interests in
       subsidiaries (this will be explained later, on page 86)
5   = PROFIT ATTRIBUTABLE TO ORDINARY SHAREHOLDERS (Often abbreviated to Profit Attributable)
     deduct dividend payable to ordinary shareholders
6   = PROFIT RETAINED (sometimes called TRANSFER TO RESERVES)

Hence the profit and loss account of a limited company might look like the example at the top of page 51. Please compare this to the sole trader's profit and loss account on page 20.

Treatment of Capital

Capital appears at the top left-hand corner of a traditional two-sided balance sheet or in the "financed by" part of a vertical balance sheet for a limited company just as it does for a sole trader. However, replacing the sole trader's simple statement is a detailed statement of the authorized and

X Co. Ltd.

Profit and Loss Account

for the year ended 31st December 19____

	£
Sales (or Turnover)	150,000
Cost of goods sold (detail as page 20)	80,000
Gross Profit	70,000
Other expenses (detail as page 20)	26,000
Operating Profit	44,000
Interest	10,000
Profit Before Taxation	34,000
Corporation tax	12,000
Profit After Taxation	22,000
Attributable to minority interests in subsidiaries	4,000
Profit Attributable to Ordinary Shareholders	18,000
Dividends	8,000
Profit Retained, transferred to reserves	£ 10,000

allotted capital and its division into shares. To this capital is now added the profit retained for the year and the total is variously called Capital and Reserves or Shareholders' Funds or Equity Interest. The following extract from the X Co. Ltd. balance sheet as at 31st December 19____ demonstrates the method:

Capital and Reserves:	£	
Authorized share capital		
10,000 6% cumulative preference shares	10,000	
90,000 ordinary shares of £1 each	90,000	
	£100,000	
		£
Called up share capital		
nil 6% cumulative preference shares		—
80,000 ordinary shares of £1 each, fully paid		80,000
	£	80,000
Profit and loss account		
Balance at end of previous year	15,000	
Add profit retained this year		
(transferred from profit and loss account)	10,000	
		25,000
Equity interest or Shareholders' Funds		105,000

Note that the amount which appears in the balance sheet for profit and loss account each year will be the cumulative balance to date. This figure is sometimes called *Reserves*.

Reserves

This is perhaps the most misleading word in the accounting language. In the English language the word conjures up an image of pots of money stashed away somewhere for a "rainy day"; this is *not* the case in the accounting language.

Reserves simply means the accumulation of profits retained and reinvested in the business over the years: hence the expression *transferred to reserves*. It is most unlikely that the reserves will be represented by a pot of money; the reserves are far more likely to have been invested in fixed assets or stock or anywhere in the net assets of the company (see a similar comment at note 5 on page 25).

Remember that *reserves* infers where the money has come from (i.e. profits retained), not where the money has gone to.

In practice the reserves in a limited company balance sheet are built up not only from retained profits transferred from the profit and loss account as in the above example but also from other "profits", for example:

—a company may revalue its properties to reflect more up-to-date market values: the "profit" on revaluation would be transferred to reserves and would no doubt be referred to as a *revaluation reserve*.

—a company may sell additional shares at a price in excess of that share's par (or face) value if the current market value is in excess of par value: the "profit" on sale of shares would be transferred to reserves and would be referred to as a *share premium account*.

If there is inadequate profit after taxation to justify a dividend in any year but the directors nevertheless feel justified in paying one, it is possible to transfer profit back to the profit and loss account from reserves for this purpose. The Companies Acts lay down strict restrictions as to which reserves can and cannot be used in this way to justify the distribution of a dividend. Hence some companies segregate their reserves into distributable and non distributable reserves.

Bonus Shares (Capitalization Issue)

As years go by and successive transfers to reserves are made, the accumulated amount of reserves obviously can become quite large in relation to the allotted capital. It is at this stage that a limited company may decide to utilize some of those reserves in "payment" for a "free" issue of shares to existing shareholders. Such an issue is called a bonus issue, or scrip issue, or capitalization issue—this latter expression recognizes that the reserves are being capitalized by the issue: i.e. an amount is transferred from reserves to capital as demonstrated below.

Suppose a company decides to make a one for two bonus issue of shares to existing shareholders: this means that for every two shares held, shareholders will be given one more "free". The impact on the capital and reserves section of the balance sheet would be as follows:

	Before the bonus issue £	After the bonus issue £
Capital and Reserves		
Allotted share capital		
ordinary shares of £1 each	100	150
Reserves	200	150
Total equity interest	300	300
(or shareholders' funds)		

Note that the total equity interest (i.e. interest of ordinary shareholders) in the company remains unchanged at £300 despite the bonus issue. All that has happened is that the disposition of the equity interest between capital and reserves has been changed. Of course the shareholder now has three shares for every two previously held but the odds are that the value of each will fall because no real value has been created for the shareholder by the bonus issue. Every shareholder previously held two shares with a market value of say £3 each (i.e. £6 value in total), but now holds three shares whose market value is now perhaps £2 each (i.e. still £6 value in total).

The tangible benefits to the shareholder from a bonus issue are:

—*if* the future dividend is maintained at the same amount *per share*, the shareholder will of course receive a higher total dividend.

—the fall in market value often stimulates market interest which might cause the market value of each share to rise above the £2 suggested above.

—having now more shares, it might be easier for shareholders to dispose of a part of their holding if they wished to do so.

Rights Issue

Do not confuse a bonus issue with a rights issue of shares. In a rights issue money does actually change hands and value is added to the company. A one for two rights issue implies that shareholders are thereby given the *right*, if they wish, to buy one new share for every two currently held.

It is unlikely that the new shares would be issued at par (i.e. their face value); they would no doubt be issued at a price slightly lower than their current market price to give shareholders some inducement to buy.

Suppose a company decides to make a one for two rights issue of £1 shares at £1.50 (say the market price is currently £1.60). The impact on the capital and reserves section of the balance sheet would be as follows:

	Before the rights issue	After the rights issue
Capital and Reserves	£	£
Allotted share capital ordinary shares of £1 each	100	150
Reserves	200	225
Total equity interest (or shareholders' funds)	300	375

Note that the allotted share capital is always shown at par value and that the 50p per share "profit on sale" (or *share premium*) is added to reserves.

Dividends

The simple statement "dividends" in X Co. Ltd.'s profit and loss account on page 51 is expanded in practice to show whether the dividend is *interim* or *final*, *paid* or *proposed* and to which class of share it applies.

Payment of dividends is governed by the Articles of Association. These usually provide that the directors may make an interim payment during the year, if justified by profits, but that they may only propose the final payment after considering an appropriate transfer to reserves. Shareholders at the annual general meeting actually declare the final dividend; however, because they cannot increase the amount proposed by the directors, this is a formality only. Because final dividends are only proposals they are unpaid at the date of the balance sheet and consequently appear amongst current liabilities when the balance sheet is prepared. The annual accounts of Typical Products Ltd. which will be discussed shortly, demonstrate these principles.

Dividends which appear in the profit and loss account are ᴜᴄᴄᴍned to be paid to shareholders net of income tax similarly to the manner in which an employer pays wages and salaries to his employees net of income tax. The amount of income tax thereby deemed to be deducted must be handed over to the Inland Revenue on a quarterly settlement. An individual shareholder who is not liable to income tax may of course claim a refund of this "tax credit" from the Inland Revenue. The amount handed over is deemed to be an advance payment of the corporation tax due on the profits from which the dividend has been declared and thus is called Advance Corporation Tax or ACT.

A *Scrip Dividend* is a dividend which is satisfied by the issue of new shares (at the current market value) instead of cash. The advantage to the company is that cash is conserved and ACT does not have to be paid (see page 191 for an explanation of ACT). The advantage to the shareholder is that small lots of shares can thereby be obtained free of any brokers fees and other transaction costs. It is quite common for companies to offer the shareholder the option of taking either cash or shares in settlement of the dividend.

Taxation

Part of the profit before taxation of a limited company will be swallowed up in taxation (predominantly Corporation Tax) and deducted in the profit and loss account as demonstrated for the X Co. Ltd. on page 51. Chapter 19 will deal with the principles of taxation but one aspect of the subject which affects company accounts must be highlighted here.

As stated above, ACT is payable quarterly. However, the balance of Corporation Tax might not become payable until, at the worst, nine months after the end of the financial year during which the taxable profits were earned; or, at the best, several years later! It is thus possible to have *two* amounts owing for Corporation Tax at the end of any financial year: the one which will become payable within one year of the balance sheet date is included amongst current liabilities but the one which might become payable beyond one year from the balance sheet date is shown separately and termed *deferred taxation*. The specimen accounts which we shall consider shortly demonstrate this situation.

Format of Annual Accounts

The Companies Acts 1985 and 1989, together with Accounting Standards, lay down the format which must be followed when a limited company prepares its annual accounts. Appendix A summarizes the provisions of the Acts.

Appendix C reproduces the annual accounts of John Waddington PLC simply as a demonstration of current practice. The reader is also encouraged to obtain a copy of the latest published annual accounts of their own company and try to understand the expressions and format used therein.

However, Appendix B reproduces the annual accounts of Typical Products Ltd. which are a simple demonstration of the principles discussed in this and earlier chapters. The meaning of most of the expressions and format used should now be understood but some new items have been introduced. So let us work through the profit and loss account and balance sheet of Typical Products Ltd. line by line, making brief comments where appropriate and making reference to earlier parts of this book which may be re-read if the meaning of a particular expression is not apparent.

Profit and Loss Account (page 206)

The general format should be reasonably understandable (ref. pp. 50–51), but the following additional comments are relevant:

the words *on ordinary activities* appear twice—this is to indicate that these items arise from normal repeating business which clearly does not apply to the *extraordinary items* which appear further down.

Attributable to minority interests in subsidiaries will be explained later (ref. pp. 85–86).

Earnings per share is yet another member of the profit family and is simply the profit attributable to Typical Products' shareholders divided by the number of shares: i.e. it is the profit (or earnings) attributable to one share.

Statement of retained profits simply reconciles the movement in the profit and loss account figure which appears in the balance sheet under capital and reserves at page 207. For simplicity in this example there has been no other movement than profit retained. In practice other items might appear there: for example see the John Waddington statement at page 212.

Statement of movement in shareholders' funds similarly reconciles the movement in the balance sheet figure at page 207.

Balance Sheet (page 207)

The vertical presentation has been adopted (ref. pp. 25). The following comments are relevant:

Tangible assets are what we have called fixed assets in earlier parts of this book (ref. pp. 23). Remember that they are shown at cost (or perhaps revaluation in the case of properties) less cumulative depreciation to date; not at current values (ref. pp. 31-33).

Current assets are those assets which are intended to be converted into cash in the normal course of business (ref. pp. 23 and 33).

Creditors—amounts falling due within one year is a fuller expression than *current liabilities* which we have used earlier (ref. pp. 23).

Taxation payable is the amount which will become payable within one year of the balance sheet date whereas *Deferred taxation*, (under provision for liabilities and charges) is the amount which might become payable beyond one year of the balance sheet date (ref. pp. 55).

Dividend payable is the proposed final dividend which cannot be paid until approved by the shareholders at the annual general meeting (ref. pp. 54).

12% Debenture 2025/2030 is borrowed money, no doubt secured on the assets of the company, which carries an obligation to pay interest at 12% p.a. and to be repaid between the years 2025 and 2030 (ref. pp. 47).

Capital and reserves, or Shareholders' funds, gives the type of detail described earlier in this chapter (ref. pp. 51–52).

Minority interests in subsidiaries will be explained later (ref. pp. 85–86).

So much for the expressions used in the annual accounts of Typical Products Ltd. But how do we set about reading these accounts and what do they tell us of the company's performance? We shall try to answer these questions in Chapter 11 but a few further matters must first be explored.

CHAPTER 7

Value Added

UP TO now we have concentrated our attention on profit and the profit and loss account as the means of measuring the effectiveness of business effort. We turn our attention briefly now to another pair of contenders for that particular crown: value added and the value added statement. What is value added and what is its role in appraising business performance?

What is Value Added?

Put in its simplest terms, value added is the difference between what we have to pay for the raw materials, supplies and services obtained from outside the firm and the amount we get from our customers for the goods we produce and the services we provide. Value added therefore represents that value we have added to bought-in supplies and services through the application of our own labour and our own equipment. Indeed it is perhaps the purest measure of wealth creation which can be devised.

Having created wealth, the next step is to consume or distribute it and in any business there are four interested parties when it comes to such distribution:

1 *employees*: whose share represents wages or salaries plus other related and fringe benefits;
2 *the government*: whose share represents taxation of all types, direct and indirect;
3 *the providers of capital*: whose share represents dividends or interest payments, plus perhaps an element of rent or hire charges;
4 *the business itself*: whose share represents retained profits and depreciation and which, like seed corn, is the vital bit representing unconsumed wealth which must be put back to ensure continued existence or growth in the future.

Significance for National Economy

If the value added of all businesses is added together, the answer is close to the Gross National Product; value added is wealth creation at a micro level, Gross National Product is wealth creation at a macro level. Indeed the first recorded use of value added was in 1790 when Mr Trenche Cox used it in the first U.S. Census of Production in order to avoid the double counting which would have occurred with any other measure of output (e.g. sales).

Successive governments tell us that if our country is to prosper we must maintain a high and productive level of Gross National Product: it seems strange, therefore, that the source of Gross National Product, i.e. value added, should have had such little emphasis in business accounting and financial reporting until relatively recently.

Significance for Productivity Measurement

If value added is (as was suggested above) the purest measure of wealth creation, then it must also be a prime candidate for effective productivity measurement. Productivity implies a comparison of outputs to inputs— value added is the output so what is the input? Input can variously be considered as people or as capital or as materials and services—whatever is regarded as the most valuable, or scarce, resource. In this context the following measures of productivity are commonly used:

1 value added per employee,
2 value added per £ of wages,
3 value added per £ of net operating assets,
4 value added per £ of materials/services input.

The matter of the most efficient utilization of a scarce resource, or limiting factor, is to be taken further in a later chapter but at present suffice to say that value added based productivity measures provide a most useful means of both inter-industry and international comparisons. And of course the comparisons can usefully be taken further by next comparing not only the creation of wealth but also its proportionate distribution between the four interested parties referred to above. Some very interesting (and often disquieting) comparisons have been published concerning the creation, distribution and retention of wealth by different companies and by different countries.

Use Within Incentive Schemes

In view of the comments made about value added as a basis for productivity measurement, it is not surprising that some firms employ value added based incentive schemes. The principle behind such schemes is that employees will earn more if they create more value added—because they receive a guaranteed *percentage share* of any such wealth created. The other three interested parties naturally will also benefit from a larger cake.

Typically such a scheme establishes a guaranteed percentage share of value added as a basis for employee remuneration. Periodically the percentage thus earned is calculated and compared to the basic remuneration already paid: any surplus is then available for bonus payment but typically only part will be paid, a smaller part (say 20%) being carried forward in reserve against future fluctuations—value added might go down as well as up!

Those who have employed value added within an incentive scheme claim that it tends to focus the mind of participants more on the creation of wealth than on its consumption: that it engenders a more responsible attitude in employees; that it is genuinely payment on delivery of productivity rather than payment on promise of productivity.

Significance in Financial Reporting

Value added is clearly a most meaningful element in financial reporting and in financial analysis although in fact it has come into popular use relatively recently, particularly when reporting to employees.

The most powerful potential application is in the publication of a Value Added Statement as an alternative to the Profit and Loss Account. The first U.K. company to take this step was Colt International Ltd. in 1974; many other companies produce a value-added statement *in addition to* the profit and loss account. A typical profit and loss account is reproduced to the left of page 61 whilst the equivalent value added statement appears to the right.

PROFIT AND LOSS ACCOUNT		VALUE ADDED STATEMENT	
	£		£
Sales	1000	Sales	1000
Production costs:		Materials and bought out services	400
Materials and services	300		
Direct labour	240	Value Added	£ 600
Depreciation	50		
Gross Profit	410	Distributed as follows:	
Admin and sales costs:		Employees	360
Materials and services	100	Government	50
Salaries	120	Providers of capital	75
Depreciation	10	Retained in the firm	115
Operating Profit	180		
Interest	20	Total value added as above	£ 600
Profit before Taxation	160		
Corporation Tax	50		
Profit after Taxation	110		
Dividend	55		
Profit Retained	£ 55		

Note that the numbers are the same; only the manner of presentation is different:

1. materials and bought out services in the value added statement of £400 is made up of £300 production materials and £100 admin etc. materials and services from the profit and loss account.

2. distribution to employees in the value added statement of £360 is made up of £240 direct labour and £120 salaries from the profit and loss account.

3. distribution to providers of capital in the value added statement of £75 is made up of £20 interest plus £55 dividend.

4. value added retained in the firm of £115 is made up of the two items of depreciation (£50 + £10) plus profit retained £55.

The arguments in favour of a value added statement revolve around putting profit and wealth creation in perspective. For example:

1. On many occasions, value added is a more meaningful basis than sales for reporting the value of output. For example: in the year following that reported above, assume production material costs increase by £100, that

this is passed directly on to the customers as increased selling price, but all other items remain the same. Sales would show an increase of 10 percent to £1100 and operating profit % sales would show a decline from £180 as percent of £1000 to £180 as percent of £1100. Surely such financial comparisons are misleading because everything that is controllable within the firm has remained unchanged. If the value added approach is used the value added will still be £600 the following year (i.e. £1100 sales minus £500 materials and bought out services) and its distribution will be unchanged.

2. The distribution of dividend to shareholders is a most emotional matter—in the example above it amounts to 50 percent of the profit after taxation. To employees this might appear excessive, yet it is a most misleading statistic because it is calculated as a percent of the last remaining piece of wealth after all others have had their share. By comparison it appears as approximately 9 percent of value added, compared to the employees' 60 percent in the value added statement presentation.

3. The true creation of wealth and its relative disposition between the four interested parties can be seen quite clearly in the value added statement. The profit and loss account does not highlight these critical subtotals.

Practical Problems

The purpose of this chapter was to give a general overview of, rather than a detailed examination of, the concept and potential use of valued added. There are practical difficulties and in particular there are considerable areas for clarification: for example, should employees' PAYE and other statutory deductions be included in the employees' share or the government's share?; is local rates a bought-out service or part of the government's share?; are rents and lease payments a bought-out service or part of the share of the providers of capital? These and other matters would seem to indicate the need for guidance and agreement, perhaps via a statement of standard accounting practice, if value added comparisons are to become really meaningful.

CHAPTER 8

Profit vs. Cash Flow

˙ ˙A FIRM goes bankrupt when it cannot meet its debts as they fall due for payment, i.e. bankruptcy is to do with a shortage of cash. However, a shortage of cash is not *necessarily* related to a shortage of profits; in fact profitable firms have been known to go bankrupt whilst firms making losses have been known to have a considerable cash surplus. This chapter explains the reasons for this apparent anomaly and explores the reasons why profit and cash flow can and do differ. These reasons give rise to the need for yet another financial document: the Cash Flow Statement.

Profit is an Opinion ...

The very first page of this book drew attention to the dual financial motive for a firm:

1. the need to make a profit in the long term,
2. the need to stay solvent in the short term.

Chapters 3 and 4 then examined in some detail what profit is and made the point that it is not a real thing but a relatively complex concept based on the application of accepted accounting rules called concepts and conventions. Furthermore, Chapter 4 pointed out that there is considerable scope for opinion in the application of these rules.

... But Cash Flow is a Fact

On the other hand, cash flow is neither complex nor a concept: it is a simple fact which reflects actual cash coming in and cash going out just as it happens without any accounting adjustments at all.

It should therefore be apparent that it would be somewhat of a coincidence if profit and cash flow were identical in amount *in any one*

63

accounting period. However, over the long-term, cumulative profit and cumulative cash flow will come closer and indeed over the whole life of a firm they will be identical in amount because the difference between the two arises from the application of accounting concepts and the passage of time.

Profit vs. Cash

The main areas where profit and cash flow will diverge can be summarized as follows:

1. *Capital expenditure*

Capital expenditure is a cash flow as and when it is paid but is charged against profit subsequently over its estimated useful working life in the form of depreciation.

It therefore follows that if capital expenditure exceeds depreciation in any accounting period, cash flow will be lower than profit by the amount of this excess ... and of course vice versa where capital expenditure is lower than depreciation.

2. *Movements in stock and work in progress*

Additions to stock and work in progress are a cash flow as and when they are paid for but are charged in arriving at profit subsequently only as they are sold.

It therefore follows that if unsold stock and work in progress increase during an accounting period, cash flow will be lower than profit by the amount of this increase ... and of course vice versa where there is a reduction in stock and work in progress.

3. *Credit Trading*

Once more the accounting concept of relevance causes the disparity between profit and cash flow. Income and expenditure go into the computation of profit at the invoice stage but are cash flows only subsequently as and when they are settled in cash.

It therefore follows that if debtors increase during an accounting period, cash flow will be lower than profit by the amount of this increase whereas if creditors increase, cash flow will be higher than profit by the amount of this increase ... and of course vice versa where there is either a decrease in debtors or in creditors.

4. Movement in Finance

Additional finance coming into the firm or repayments of borrowing by the firm are clearly cash flows but of themselves have no impact on profit because they affect only the balance sheet.

It is the interaction between these four areas which is at the heart of the difference between profit and cash flow. One of the unfortunate facts of business life is that the first three of these areas all tend to work in the same direction once triggered off. For example, whilst a firm is expanding:

1. capital expenditure will almost certainly exceed depreciation,
2. and stock and work in progress will increase,
3. and debtors and creditors will increase,

and therefore profitable expansion could well be accompanied by an acutely negative cash flow unless creditors exceed debtors by a considerable amount (as they do in a cash-and-carry operation). This manifestation is known as "overtrading", i.e. expansion without due consideration for the negative cash flow and the consequential additional capital thereby required. Overtrading is a frequent cause of bankruptcy and kills many a promising young enterprise.

The impact of inflation on cash flow is identical to that of expansion: i.e. (with the exclusion of cash and carry operations) an acutely negative cash flow and consequential additional capital requirements. We shall return to this problem in the next chapter.

Cash Flow from Operations

In Chapter 6 we introduced the term operating profit—this is the profit earned from normal business operations or trading activities. We will now consider the cash flow generated from those same activities.

Let us begin with an oversimplified profit and loss account of a firm with only cash business, i.e. no credit trading:

	£
Cash sales	900
Deduct: cash expenses*	600
depreciation	200
Operating profit	£ 100

* Includes materials, labour, rates, heating, etc.

Note that depreciation is not an actual cash expense but is an accounting adjustment. It therefore follows that, although operating profit is £100, cash flow from operations is £300 (i.e. £900-£600).

Alternatively accountants arrive at this figure of £300 by adding together operating profit and depreciation (i. e. £100 + £200 in our example above): this is logical because depreciation is a non-cash item and therefore must be added back to operating profit to reveal the net effect of the genuine cash items excluding depreciation.

Cash flow from operations therefore starts its life as operating profit plus depreciation. (Depreciation is the normal non-cash charge made against operating profit; if there are any other peculiar non-cash charges then these also would be added back to operating profit in arriving at cash flow from operations.)

However, although depreciation is not a cash payment, capital expenditure certainly is. If, in addition to the cash expenses of £600 in the above example, there had also been capital expenditure of £250 then cash flow from operations would have come down to only £50 from its starting point of £300 (see area 1 on page 64). And what if £40 more stock had been bought in cash than had been used and charged in arriving at operating profit . . . cash flow from operations would now come down to £10 although operating profit would still be £100 (see area 2 on page 64). Furthermore if part of those sales of £900 represent uncollected credit sales and part of those expenses of £600 represent unpaid credit purchases then the actual cash flow from operations will end up a very different number indeed (see area 3 on page 64).

So our terminology needs refining. Operating profit plus depreciation is best defined as *Potential Cash Flow From Operations* (i.e. the cash flow which would have been generated from operations had there been no capital expenditure, stock movement or credit trading). *Actual Cash Flow From Operations* will then be measured as follows:

Operating profit
plus depreciation

equals Potential Cash Flow from Operations

Minus capital expenditure
plus proceeds of sales of fixed assets

plus or minus movements in working capital as follows:
  minus increase in stocks and work in progress
  or plus decrease in stocks and work in progress

  minus increase in debtors
  or plus decrease in debtors

  plus increase in creditors
  or minus decrease in creditors

equals Actual Cash Flow from Operations

Non-Operating Cash Flows

In addition to cash flow from operations, the following further, non-operating cash flows may occur:

Inflows of Cash

1. New sources of finance—either from sale of shares or from borrowing.
2. Any other non-operating income—e.g. dividends or interest received.

Outflows of Cash

1. Contractual financial obligations—e.g.:
   interest paid on borrowing
   repayment of borrowing
   payments due under finance leases or hire purchase

2. Appropriations of profit—
   taxation payment
   dividend payment

Cash Flow Statement

We have now established that profit and cash flow can be very different in amount and so it is obvious that, in measuring business performance, we cannot look only at profit and how it has arisen; we must also look at cash flow and how *it* has arisen. So, in addition to the profit and loss account (or its variant the value added statement), we need another document which summarizes the cash flow position and identifies its various elements as described above. Such a document is called a Cash Flow Statement, or Funds Flow Statement or indeed Statement of Source and Application of Funds. (There is a fine academic distinction between "cash" and "funds" which this author chooses to ignore.)

One example of a cash flow statement appears on page 208 for Typical Products Ltd; this statement should now be understandable. Note that although Typical Products Ltd. has made a profit, it has had a considerably negative cash flow this year causing its net borrowings to increase dramatically.

Unfortunately in practice there are several different ways of setting out this Statement because the history of the Cash Flow Statement is relatively short in the U.K. The profit and loss account was first developed in 1494 (see page 11); the statement of source and application of funds came in in 1976 with SSAP 10 (see page 40); whereas the Cash Flow Statement only came in in 1992 with FRS 1 (see page 40). The Format appearing at page 214 for John Waddington PLC follows the recommended approach of FRS 1.

Our review of the major summarizing accounting documents is now complete; there are four in all, each interrelated:

1. the static document called a Balance Sheet,
supported by three link documents which explain changes which have taken place between two balance sheet dates; two of them explain movements in profits or "reserves":

2. the Profit and Loss Account,

3. the Value Added Statement,
whilst the other explains movement in cash or net borrowings:

4. the Cash Flow Statement.

CHAPTER 9

Impact of Inflation on Accounting Information

ACCOUNTING is concerned with recording and measuring business performance and uses money as its measuring device. But money is not stable: its value fluctuates due to the impact of inflation. What does this imply for accounting information? In this chapter we seek both to answer this question and briefly to review the history and current state of accounting attitudes and practice. The chapter in no way attempts to be an economics treatise on the causes and cure of inflation.

Impact of Inflation on Profit

If I begin an accounting period with an item in stock which cost £10 and during that period I sell it for £16 cash, it is obvious that I have made £6 operating profit. If I have to pay half the profit in tax and decide to pay the other half in dividend (i.e. £3 each) I will now be left with £10 in cash with which I can replenish my stock and so stay in business for the next accounting period.

The process can be summarized as follows:

	Profit position £	Cash position £
Sales	16	+ 16
Less cost of stock consumed	10	
Operating profit	6	
Less tax	3	− 3
dividend	3	− 3
Profit retained	Nil	
Cash in hand for stock replacement		£10

... and of course this can go on repeating itself year after year *ad infinitum* ... or until inflation strikes!

Now suppose that *at the time of sale* the replacement value of the stock, which still originally cost £10, is now £12 and I still sell for £16: how much operating profit have I made? There are in fact two possible answers to this deceptively simple question:

1. £6 as before, i.e. the difference between selling price and original cost of stock sold. This is the answer that would be given by *historical cost accounting*.
2. £4; i.e. the difference between selling price and replacement value, at the date of sale, of the stock sold. This is the answer that would be given by *current cost accounting*.

The problem with historical cost accounting is that if tax and dividend are based on an operating profit of £6, we have seen above that this leaves cash in hand of £10—and if stock replacement now costs £12 I will either have to reduce my level of activity to something which costs only £10 or else I shall have to borrow £2—not to expand but just to stand still. On the other hand, if tax and dividend are based on a current cost operating profit of £4 I can still afford to carry on my business and remain self-financing as follows:

	Profit position £	Cash position £
Sales	16	+ 16
Less replacement value of stock consumed	12	
Current cost operating profit	4	
Less tax	2	− 2
dividend	2	− 2
Profit retained	Nil	
Cash in hand for stock replacement		£12

This is a grossly over-simplified example, of course, but is reasonably representative of the situation which exists for any firm which charges, in arriving at profit, for the consumption of assets which subsequently have to be replaced. The prime examples are stock replacement and fixed asset replacement (similarly to the above example: a depreciation charge based on the original cost of fixed assets will provide an inadequate basis for ultimate replacement and will over-state profits in the meantime). The longer the time delay between replacement dates, the more marked is the over-statement of profits if inflation continues; heavy engineering, for example, is particularly vulnerable here.

Impact of Inflation on Cash Flow

Profit is only a concept (albeit an important one) and therefore it can be said to be only academic to worry about the over statement of profit. However, cash flow is a reality and the need for an additional £2 in the example above is certainly not academic! This is the real killer as far as inflation is concerned: is the firm able to generate sufficient cash flow from its ongoing operations to enable it to replace its assets as they are consumed without recourse to additional finance, i.e. without recourse to the need to borrow just to stand still?

In the mid-1970s when inflation in the U.K. was running very high, many firms found themselves in acute financial difficulty. The reason for this is not difficult to establish. Refer back to page 65 where the cash flow consequences of expansion were explained. Now forget about expansion: just consider the cash flow consequences of standing still in a period of inflation. How much more cash will be required by a firm to cover an inflationary uplift in both the cost of replacing fixed assets and the maintenance of working capital? For all but a cash-and-carry operation the amount could be considerable. And if the inflationary uplift in potential cash flow from operations is inadequate to meet this additional cash requirement, there will be a negative pressure on actual cash flow from operations which may have to be financed by costly borrowing.

Even when the *annual* rate of inflation is very low, the *cumulative* impact of inflation on the replacement value of longer lived fixed assets or of stocks held for lengthy maturation could cause cash flow problems.

Rate of Inflation

There is no one universal measure of inflation. Different countries, different industries, different firms, different categories of income and expenditure within the same firm all suffer different rates of inflation and this is one of the problems when accounting for inflation. How shall it be measured? A general measure which is available in the U.K. is the Index of

Retail Prices and the graph below reveals the trend in this index over a period of time.

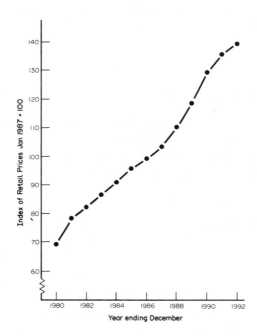

Because the Index of Retail Prices will not be appropriate to all firms, clearly it is desirable for each firm to identify and measure the specific impact of inflation within its own activities as a necessary prerequisite to assessing the impact of inflation on its own financial performance.

Inflation and Financial Performance

Before going on to review the history and development of accounting for inflation let us pause to summarize the problem. If the falling value of money caused by inflation is not taken into account, the practical impact upon a company via its traditional financial statements will manifest itself in one or all of the following ways:

as highlighted in the earlier example—

(a) Over-statement of profits due to under charge of certain expenditures (principally depreciation and withdrawals from stock).

(b) Over-distribution of dividends out of the over-stated profits created at (a).

(c) Inability to finance replacement of assets due to over distribution of profits at (b) and to the excessive tax charge (which traditionally ignores inflation).

But also—

(d) Understatement of the real value of assets employed in the business (because historical cost accounting traditionally bases the balance-sheet valuation of assets on cost).

(e) Gross over-statement of return on investment (or return on assets) due to the relationship between (a) and (d).

(f) Complacent attitude towards growth trends (suppose our sales or profit graph followed the same upward moving line as in the graph on page 72: has there *really* been growth?)

(g) Ill-founded belief that profits are "excessive".

Monetary Items

In accounting for inflation, one thorny matter has to be grasped: how to deal with monetary items. Monetary items are amounts fixed by reality, contract or statute in terms of numbers of pounds: there are both monetary assets (e.g. cash and debtors) and monetary liabilities (e.g. creditors and most loans).

To hold monetary assets over a period of time is to suffer a loss in *purchasing power* (but not of actual £ notes) whereas to owe monetary liabilities over a period of time is to reap a gain in *purchasing power* (but not in actual £ notes). On the other hand, to hold *non*-monetary assets (e.g. stocks and fixed assets) is to suffer a loss in actual £ notes, as demonstrated in the simple example earlier in this chapter, when it comes to replacement of those assets.

Should accounting for inflation take account of the loss or gain on monetary items despite the fact that it is not a real loss or gain in terms of £ notes? Consider a bank (full of the monetary asset cash) at one end of the spectrum and a well-borrowed company (i.e. with significant monetary liabilities) at the other end of the spectrum. The difference in reported profit could be considerable as revealed by the following extracts from a review carried out in 1973 by the London brokers Phillips & Drew at a time when inflation was roaring away:

Company	Year end	Conventional pre-tax profit	Estimated pre-tax profit adjusted for inflation	
			ignoring monetary items	with monetary adjustments
		(£m)	(£m)	(£m)
Barclays Bank	Dec. 74	162	153	95
Grand Metropolitan	Sept. 74	33	5	99
Tube Investments	Dec. 74	40	(15)	1
Tesco	Feb. 75	23	11	24

... and as highlighted by the significant 1977 Ford Motor Co. U.K. wage claim: how much can the company afford to pay? How much profit has been made?

Ford (post-tax)	Dec. 76	59	5.6	67

History of Accounting for Inflation

So what has the Accounting Profession been doing about inflation, what does it recommend for dealing with the problem? This section very briefly traces the significant dates and cast of characters in the unfolding history of accounting for inflation in the U.K.:

January 1949

The Institute of Charactered Accountants published its recommendation on accounting for changes in the purchasing power of money but this carried little weight and had little impact. In any event the rate of inflation was relatively low.

August 1971

The Accounting Standards Committee (ASC) published a discussion paper entitled "Inflation and Accounts".

January 1973

Following its discussion paper the ASC issued an exposure draft (ED8) which, if accepted, was to become a statement of standard accounting practice (SSAP) with effect from January 1974.

July 1973

The government asked the ASC to hold their fire because it was setting up its own committee to conduct an enquiry into inflation accounting under the chairmanship of Francis Sandilands.

May 1974

The ASC nevertheless published an amended ED8 as a *provisional* SSAP7 to apply to published accounts for periods beginning after 30th June 1974. PSSAP7 was simple: it recommended the publication of a supplementary statement which uplifted all the figures in the profit and loss account and balance sheet by reference to the retail price index. The method was to be called CPP (Constant, or Current, Purchasing Power) and, because it uplifted all figures, automatically adjusted for monetary items.

September 1975

Came the bombshell. The Sandilands Committee reported: it rejected CPP as being insufficiently appropriate to an individual firm; it dismissed the monetary items adjustment; it recommended a system of adjustment based on individual replacement values to be called CCA (Current Cost Accounting); it recommended that the adjustment process be taken right down into the book-keeping and that a steering group be set up to hammer out the details.

January 1976

The steering group recommended by Sandilands was set up under Douglas Morpeth charged with producing a workable system of CCA to be operational by 24th December 1977.

November 1976

After displaying considerable speed Morpeth published, via the ASC, ED18: "Current Cost Accounting". ED18 was a necessarily complex document, virtually rewriting the concepts upon which accounting had stood for almost 500 years. It was open for discussion up to 31st May 1977 whereafter the final SSAP was to become operational in stages between July 1978 and January 1980. An impossible timetable it subsequently transpired.

July 1977

Came the revolution! ED18 never became an SSAP: a groundswell of professional accounting opinion thought it was impractical, too subjective and too complicated. Its fate was finally sealed at a Special Meeting of the English Institute of Chartered Accountants which rejected ED18 and the whole concept of a *compulsory* system of CCA. The ASC reacted quickly to this rejection and on the rebound set up yet another working party, under the chairmanship of William Hyde, charged with the task of producing something as quickly as possible which would be simple, speedy, inexpensive and, above all, practical and operationally acceptable to accountants and account users alike.

November 1977

Hyde completed his deliberations and the "Hyde Guidelines" were produced as an interim measure pending a fuller reconsideration of ED18. Hyde required all companies listed on the Stock Exchange to include in their published accounts a prominent statement showing three adjustments to profit computed under the historical cost accounting convention: depreciation adjustment, cost of sales adjustment and gearing adjustment (these expressions will be explained later).

April 1979

Morpeth's fuller reconsideration was published as ED24.

March 1980

SSAP16, "Currrent Cost Accounting" was published with a suggestion that it be let stand for a trial period of at least 3 years during which time firms would gain experience in its use and experiment as necesssary. SSAP16 applied to quoted public limited companies and required the production of a separate current cost profit and loss account and balance sheet in addition to the historical cost ones. However, historical cost accounting was to remain.

July 1982

Came the second revolution! The same faction which led the 1977 revolution came back demanding the scrapping of SSAP16. The Institute of Chartered Accountants won this time but by the most slender of majorities and so felt it necessary to instruct the ASC to return once more to the drawing board to have a substitute for SSAP16 ready when its trial period came to an end.

July 1984

Amidst continuing dissention and debate, and against the backcloth of falling rates of inflation, ED35 "Accounting for the Effects of Changing Prices" was published. The proposals in ED35 were a considerable watering down of SSAP16: the current cost balance sheet was dropped and the profit and loss account adjustments could be lost somewhere in the notes to the accounts if desired.

1985—CCA RIP

But even the watered down ED35 could not gain unanimous support and in March 1985 it was withdrawn. The Stock Exchange no longer required compliance with SSAP16 and in May 1985 the ASC announced that SSAP16 was no longer mandatory. Noises are being made that "something must be done" but at the time of writing there is no great enthusiasm for the subject.

And so it is that after more than 15 years of costly experimentation and debate, firms are back to where they were: they can publish inflation accounting information or not as they wish and in whatever form they choose. The Companies Act 1989 does permit the use of CCA reporting, provided that corresponding historical cost information appears in the notes to the accounts. The published accounting policies will prominently state which accounting convention has been used; see for example page 216 "The group accounts are prepared . . . under the historical cost convention".

Current Cost Accounting (CCA)

The philosophy of current cost accounting rests on the simple statement:
"the first bit of profit doesn't count"
because, just to stand still in times of inflation, some of the profit ought to be set aside to provide for replacement of assets before deciding how much is available for distribution as dividend. This is clearly demonstrated in the simple example on page 70 where £2 was required to replace stock consumed: failure to set aside this amount dictated that £2 had to be borrowed just to stand still.

So those firms which try to reflect the impact of inflation when publishing their accounts will no doubt do it by some variation of the following four adjustments. The first three would affect the operating profit, the fourth is a non-operating item:

1. *Depreciation adjustment*:
   This is the difference between the depreciation computed on the original (historical) cost of fixed assets and the depreciation which would have been computed on the current cost of equivalent fixed assets if they had been replaced at the balance sheet date.

2. *Cost of sales adjustment (COSA)*:
   This is the difference between the original (historical) cost of stock and work in progress consumed and the current cost of that same stock and work in progress if it had to be replaced at its date of consumption (e.g. the £2 difference in the simple example which began this chapter).

3. *Monetary working capital adjustment (MWCA)*:
   This reflects the impact of inflation on the amount of capital tied up in monetary working capital (principally debtors minus creditors); as inflation moves up, so must the value of debtors minus creditors which thus creates the need for a further investment of an amount approximating to this monetary working capital adjustment.

4. *Gearing adjustment*:
   This is that proportion of the first three adjustments which has not actually been suffered by shareholders because they have used other people's money (substantially borrowings) instead of their own to finance the investment in fixed assets, stock and work in progress and monetary working capital.

Where Are We Now?

CCA may be dead but inflation is not necessarily so! Moreover inflation does not have a constant universal impact: some areas, some activities, sometimes suffer more from inflation than others. Therefore, irrespective of what the accounting profession is or is not doing with *published* information, every operating manager needs to know how inflation affects his own planning and control decisions and so he must have inflation corrected *management* information on a regular basis.

The reader is invited to ascertain his or her own firm's policies and practice regarding the impact of inflation on both published and management accounting information.

CHAPTER 10

Published Financial Information

THE general form and content of the annual accounts of a limited company have been considered in earlier chapters.

The actual form, content and degree of detail of any particular set of *internal accounts* depends on the wishes and whims of the directors and management for whom these accounts are prepared as internal documents of control. Should any further information be required, it can readily be ascertained from the books of account.

However, directors have a duty to account for their stewardship to members of the company and, in view of the remarks made above about the contents of internal accounts, it is not surprising that the law sets out certain minimum information which must be disclosed in any *published* accounts circulated *externally* to shareholders.

Moreover, there is an increasing weight of legal and social pressure to present financial and other information to wider groups of interested parties over and above the shareholder/investor group.

Legal Requirements

The prime legal requirement for presentation of financial information by limited companies is embodied in the Companies Acts which state that once at least in every calendar year every limited company shall present to shareholders and file with the Registrar of Companies a set of annual accounts which give a true and fair view of the company's affairs. The Acts stipulate in some detail the *minimum* information which shall be disclosed in or with these accounts and Appendix A to this book is included to demonstrate the detail called for in the Companies Acts 1985 and 1989.

Some companies take the opportunity to present more than the legal minimum information, in particular when producing the profit and loss account. For this reason the reader of a published profit and loss account must note with care words such as "gross profit", "trading profit", "surplus on trading" and "operating profit" to understand exactly what the company means by these expressions and how they relate to this book's family of profits introduced on page 50. However, due to the universal application of the provisions of the Acts, there is an increasing degree of consistency and comparability between the published accounts of limited companies.

The requirements of earlier Companies Acts were rooted in the concept that shareholders and debentureholders were the only parties interested in, and therefore entitled to receive financial information. Later Companies Acts have broadened this narrow view but more particularly other pieces of legislation (e.g. the Industry Act, the Health & Safety at Work Act) have progressively added to the legal requirement for publication of financial information to a wider audience.

Legal requirements are no longer parochially national and, in addition to publishing financial and other information required by U.K. legislation, U.K. companies must also comply with EC legislation and directives. The OECD also has specific requirements for the publication of financial information by multinational enterprises.

Other Pressures

The legislature tends to follow a leisurely process, brings in changes infrequently and often follows rather than dictates public opinion and best practice. When a company publishes financial and other information it is therefore under much greater pressures than merely legal. Some of the further pressures which might also help to shape the form and content of published financial information are as follows:

1. *Stock Exchange Requirements*

If a public company wishes to continue its listing and so retain its quotation it must fulfil the current requirements of the body which governs the appropriate stock exchange (the Stock Exchange Council in the U.K.). Such requirements may cover not only content but also frequency of publication of information: for example, a company quoted on the U.K. Stock Exchange must publish an Interim Statement half-way through the year in addition to its annual published accounts; some other stock exchanges require the publication of quarterly information.

2. *Statements of Standard Accounting Practice*

Chapter 4 discussed the development of EDs, SSAPs and FRSs and their implication when a company publishes its annual accounts.

3. *Government Green and White Papers*

Government views in anticipation of pending legislation clearly exert some pressure.

4. *Developing Accounting Thought*

Other influences create renewed thought and reconsideration in the accounting field, for example the Cadbury Committee report on corporate governance, the Accounting Standard Board publication of discussion documents, particularly in its developing statement of principles on the preparation of financial statements.

5. *Competition*

Each year the magazine *The Accountant* (the journal of the English Institute of Chartered Accountants) presents two awards for what are judged by a panel to be the best set of published accounts submitted by a large and a small quoted company. This does tend to create a spirit of competition which has done much to raise the general standard of presentation and disclosure. Other competitions are also run in the area of presentation of information to employees.

6. *Best Practice*

There will always be leaders and followers in any activity and the presentation of financial information is no exception. Some accountants feel that the pace of development in the accounting profession is not fast enough and so "do their own thing"; pressure groups are formed; papers are produced: therefore some companies will always disclose more than others. No doubt this process will continue into the future as radical developments of today become the accepted commonplace of tomorrow.

The Published Report and Accounts Booklet

Having considered the legal requirements and other pressures summarized above, the board of a public limited company must decide upon the precise nature and content of its published financial information. This will be put together in the form of an *Annual Report and Accounts* booklet. The precise layout of the contents of this booklet vary from company to company but generally adopts the following sequence:

1. Names of directors, secretary and auditor of the company and address of the registered office.

2. Notice convening the annual general meeting, incorporating the agenda, which will contain five items:

to receive and consider the director's report and annual accounts;

to approve the proposed dividends;

to elect directors;

to fix the remuneration of the auditors;

to transact any other business which can properly be dealt with at an annual general meeting.

3. Summarized financial highlights of the year.

4. Chairman's statement, which reviews the activities of the company, assesses progress in the context of the national and international political and economic climate and forecasts future prospects.

5. Report of the directors, which recommends how the profit shall be appropriated and gives various information required by the Acts (see, for example, Appendix A).

6. Statement of accounting policies which clarifies the company's attitude towards its interpretation and application of accounting concepts and standards discussed in Chapter 4.

7. Published annual accounts generally prepared under the historical cost accounting convention and comprising:

consolidated profit and loss account;

consolidated balance sheet;

parent company balance sheet;

cash flow statement;

value added statement (in some cases);

notes to the accounts giving further detail as necessary

8. Report of the auditors on the published accounts.

9. Financial and other statistical summaries in diagrammatic or tabular form, indicating the progress of the company over the past 5 or 10 years,

or amplifying certain figures contained in the published accounts or giving segmental information.

10. Any other detailed information on the activities of the company which may be of interest to readers—often using full colour illustrations, photographic reproductions and other commercial art forms.

Appendix C is an extract from the published report and accounts booklet of John Waddington PLC and is included as an example of the type of information published under items 6–8 above.

Consolidated Accounts

One of the requirements of the Acts is that when a company has subsidiaries, consolidated accounts shall be prepared embracing the activities of both parent and subsidiary companies. Parent and subsidiaries are collectively known as a *group of companies* and consolidated accounts are sometimes called *group accounts*.

Consider the following abbreviated balance sheet of *P* Ltd.:

	£	£
Fixed assets		
Tangible assets		100
Investment in S Ltd.: Shares	10,000	
Loan	2,000	12,000
		12,100
Current assets	400	
Current liabilities	200	
Net current assets		200
Net assets		£ 12,300
Called up share capital		11,000
Reserves		1,300
Shareholders' funds		£ 12,300

It is obvious that the substance of *P* Ltd. is sunk in *S* Ltd.; unless members of *P* Ltd. have some indication of the value of this investment, they are unable to assess the financial position of *P* Ltd.

S Ltd. is a wholly owned subsidiary of *P* Ltd., and its abbreviated balance sheet is as follows:

	£	£
Fixed assets		
Tangible assets		17,300
Current assets	1,100	
Current liabilities	1,000	
Net current assets		100
Total assets less current liabilities		17,400
Deduct loan from P Ltd.		2,000
Net assets		£ 15,400
Called up share capital		10,000
Reserves		5,400
Shareholders' funds		£ 15,400

P has invested £10,000 in S Ltd. which is represented by net assets employed in S Ltd. now valued, for balance-sheet purposes, at £15,400. Net assets of P Ltd. (and hence shareholders' funds) of £12,300 are consequently understated by £5,400.

A consolidated balance sheet shows the total net assets employed in the group controlled by the parent company. For the investment in a subsidiary appearing in the balance sheet of the parent company is substituted the actual net assets representing that investment. A simple way of doing this is to add together the balance sheets of both parent and subsidiary companies, allowing the investment in subsidiary in the one balance sheet to cancel out the called up share capital in the other. The consolidated balance sheet of P Ltd. and its subsidiary would be as follows:

	£	£
Fixed assets		
Tangible assets (100 + 17,300)		17,400
Current assets (400 + 1100)	1,500	
Current liabilities (200 + 1000)	1,200	
Net current assets		300
Net assets of the Group		£ 17,700
Called up share capital of P Ltd.		11,000
Reserves (1300 + 5400)		6,700
Shareholders' funds		£ 17,700

This balance sheet now shows the full balance sheet value of net assets employed in the group as a whole, £17,700, and gives to the members of P Ltd. a clearer indication of the use to which their capital has been put. Observe that the loan between P Ltd. and S Ltd. cancels out in the aggregation of the two balance sheets and does not appear in the consolidated balance sheet. This is reasonable because it is an intra group matter and does not affect the overall financial position of the group.

A consolidated profit and loss account would similarly be prepared for publication by aggregating each item in the profit and loss accounts of parent and subsidiary companies and eliminating intra group items.

Consolidated Accounts with Minority Interests

In the preceding section, S Ltd. was a wholly owned subsidiary of P Ltd. Had P Ltd. owned only 80 percent of the shares in S Ltd., the other 20 percent would be owned by shareholders outside the group, who are known as *outside shareholders* or *minority interests*. Despite a subsidiary being only partly owned, a consolidated balance sheet is still required if the overall financial position of the group is to be revealed.

Consider now the situation where the balance sheet of P Ltd. is as before (page 83) but the balance sheet of S Ltd. (now 80 percent owned) is as follows:

	£	£
Fixed assets		
Tangible assets		20,200
Current assets	1,800	
Current liabilities	1,500	
Net current assets		300
Total assets less current liabilities		20,500
Deduct loan from P Ltd.		2,000
Net assets		£ 18,500
Called up share capital		12,500
Reserves		6,000
Shareholders' funds		£ 18,500

Net assets are valued at £18,500 in this balance sheet of which 80 percent, or £14,800, is owned by *P* Ltd. and 20 percent, or £3,700, by minority interests. The £10,000 investment by *P* Ltd. is thus now represented by net assets employed in *S* Ltd., which are valued, for balance sheet purposes, at £14,800—net assets of *P* Ltd. are consequently understated by £4,800.

How shall a consolidated balance sheet be prepared when a subsidiary is not wholly owned? In this example, 80 percent only of the net assets of *S* Ltd. could be aggregated with those of *P* Ltd., but this method would become complicated when there were many subsidiaries to consolidate. Furthermore, this method would not reveal the full extent of net assets employed in the group. The method adopted in practice is to aggregate all the net assets as for wholly owned subsidiaries but then show, in the consolidated balance sheet, that part financed by minority interests in subsidiaries. The consolidated balance sheet will then usefully show where the money has come from to run the whole group (including that provided by outsiders) and the disposition of these funds about the group. Our consolidated balance sheet will thus be:

	£	£
Fixed assets		
Tangible assets (100 + 20,200		20,300
Current assets (400 + 1,800)	2,200	
Current liabilities (200 + 1,500)	1,700	
Net current assets		500
Net assets of the group		£ 20,800
Called up share capital of *P* Ltd.		11,000
Reserves (1,300 + 80% of 6,000)		6,100
Shareholders' funds		17,100
Minority interests in subsidiaries		
(20% of 18,500)		3,700
Total financing of the group		£ 20,800

A consolidated profit and loss account would be prepared as described on page 84 and then the proportion of profit attributable to minority interests would be deducted, leaving a net amount available to the parent company—which will agree with the amount incorporated in the consolidated balance sheet. (See for example page 206 and page 207).

Associated, or Related, Companies

A subsidiary company is one in which a parent company holds a controlling interest (i.e. more than 50 percent of the voting shares). In this case the whole of the items from the net assets and from the profit and loss account of each subsidiary are aggregated into the consolidated accounts of the group, a deduction being made at the end for that part attributable to minority interests in subsidiaries: as described in the previous section of this chapter.

An *associated company*, or *related company*, is one in which there is a substantial, but not a controlling interest by another company. "Substantial" is most frequently defined as between 20 percent and 50 percent of the voting shares. Because there is no control, it would be quite wrong to go through the aggregation process described above for subsidiary companies: the totals thus produced would be meaningless. The normal practice for dealing with results of associated, or related, companies in a set of published accounts therefore is as follows:

1. in the consolidated profit and loss account: the relevant share only of the profit before taxation and of the tax charge of the related company are shown.
2. in the consolidated balance sheet: the original cost of the investment in the related company only is shown.
3. fuller details might be given in the notes to the published accounts if the company thought fit to do so.

So above 50 percent is a subsidiary company (i.e. control); 20 percent to 50 percent is an associated, or related, company (i.e. a substantial say but short of control) ... therefore what about an investment in another company of less than 20 percent of its voting shares? Such an investment is often termed a *trade investment* or *other investment* and treatment in the consolidated accounts is very simple:

1. only the income (interest or dividend) received is shown in the consolidated profit and loss account.
2. only the original cost of the investment is shown in the consolidated balance sheet.

Presentation of Financial Information to Employees

The 1970s saw a great movement towards industrial democracy and one of the manifestations of this was the increasing legal and other pressures, referred to at p. 80, towards the greater disclosure of financial information to employees. If a company decides to go down this particular path it is opening a great big Pandora's Box because it must now decide such matters as how far down the line to present, what to present, how, when, in what form and with what frequency.

In certain cases there has been an attempt to tailor the published report and accounts booklet so as to cater both for the shareholder and the employee. However, in the majority of cases, those companies which do present financial information to employees do so in a special Employees' Report which generally presents information in an abbreviated, simplified and less legalistic format which concentrates on those aspects of a company's performance deemed to be of greater interest to employees. Some companies back up this document with specially prepared films or other audio visual material.

Summary Financial Statements

The legal and other pressures referred to in this chapter do tend to produce thicker and more technically complex financial statements which, it might be argued, go far beyond the ability of the small shareholder to comprehend. Not unnaturally, therefore, following on the success of the presentation of financial information to employees, there was a movement urging a similar presentation of simplified financial information to shareholders.

The Companies Act 1989 gave permission for the first time for shareholders to be given the opportunity of opting, if they wish, to receive a Summary Financial Statement. This is derived from the full published accounts, is accompanied by an auditor's statement and is of course much more readable; however, it must incorporate a "health warning" that the summary financial statement does not contain sufficient information to allow for a full understanding of the results of the group.

Having now been introduced to the wealth of published financial information which is available from a public limited company in particular, how does one use this information to determine whether the financial performance of the company is good or bad? This will be the purpose of the next two chapters.

CHAPTER 11

Interpretation of Annual Accounts

IN EARLIER chapters we have considered both the way in which annual accounts are prepared and the information they contain. This chapter is concerned with reading these accounts and understanding the story they tell.

First Principles

Anyone reading accounts must bear in mind certain basic facts if the reading is to be performed at all intelligently:

1. Any product of an accounting system suffers from the severe limitations discussed in Chapter 1 and is based on the conventions and concepts discussed in Chapter 4.

2. Figures are mere symbols on a piece of paper and the "bigness" or "smallness" of a figure is meaningless unless considered in its context: therefore ratios and trends must be developed in order to assess one figure in the light of another.

3. Invalid comparisons are dangerous but easily made when two figures have been computed on different bases. The golden rule is always to compare like with like.

Points of View

Whilst a set of figures can tell only one story, each reader will be particularly interested in one special aspect and will therefore slant his interpretation in that direction. Examples of biased interpretation of facts are seen every day in "authentic" reports appearing in different national newspapers—what *sort* of facts does the reader wish to know? What do *you* wish to know from a set of accounts?

A reader's attitude of mind or particular interest must colour his interpretation, which will differ from that of a reader with other interests.

Management, for example, is interested in detailed control of operations and seeks to make the business more successful. A shareholder or prospective shareholder looks to the security of the investment, the anticipated return and the prospects for capital growth. The bank manager, or other person advancing a loan, is more concerned with security, ability to pay interest and ease of repayment. A creditor's prime considerations are getting paid and obtaining further orders. Take-over bidders will look for undeveloped potential, or activities and possessions which can be economically combined with their own, or saleable assets ("asset stripping").

The object of this chapter is to acquaint the reader with certain techniques of interpretation of accounts. The degree of importance placed upon each technique must depend on the purpose for which the interpretation is being made.

Non-financial Considerations

Financial interpretation of accounts can never constitute a complete review of a business: many other non-quantitative appraisals must be made. What size and stage has the business reached? What type of business is being carried on? What does the future hold: technologically, economically and politically? These are just a few of the questions which may have to be answered before the interpretation is complete. Such considerations are outside the field of accounting; the financial interpretation only is considered here.

What to Look For

Financial interpretation is concerned with a firm's financial health—both presently and in prospect. Pointers which will help this interpretation are as follows:

1. Operating efficiency—i.e. how efficiently is the business being run by its operating managers; this has three aspects:
   (a) operating profitability
   (b) asset productivity, or efficient use of resources
   (c) cash flow (although this is largely determined by (a) and (b))
2. Liquidity—i.e. can the business pay its way
3. Financial structure—i.e. is the split of financing between shareholders and borrowing sensible and safe

4. Shareholder satisfaction—i.e. is the shareholder happy? this has three aspects:
   (a) shareholder profitability
   (b) dividend
   (c) share value

As a demonstration of financial interpretation we shall shortly apply these pointers to the published accounts of Typical Products Ltd., extracts from which are reproduced at Appendix B. However, we must first establish certain principles concerning the measurement of profitability.

Operating Management Responsibility

The profit and loss account and balance sheet are made up of a mixture of operating and non-operating items. Therefore if we are to assess correctly the financial performance of operating management it is first necessary to isolate from the profit and loss account and balance sheet those four areas for which operating management is responsible:

1. the revenue generated by operations
2. the profit made on that revenue
3. the resources employed to make that profit and generate that revenue
4 the cash flow generated by these operations

Clear definition of these areas of responsibility is necessary so that every operating manager is made aware of the precise basis for his or her performance appraisal. Furthermore, a uniform definition is necessary to ensure consistency when comparing the financial performance of different operating managers or different companies.

Each company must define its own terms and develop its own house rules as to performance appraisal; clearly different companies and different financial analysts might employ different definitions. For the purpose of financial analysis in this book, the author's personal preference will be used as follows:

revenue generated:
   — sales (or turnover) but excluding VAT, sales tax and excise duties because these do not reflect operating management's decisions
profit made:
   — operating profit (see page 50): this reflects normal operating decisions

because it is the profit before adding non-operating income (e.g. investment income received) and before deducting non-operating expenses (i.e. interest, tax and dividend) and before extraordinary items

resources employed:
— only those assets controlled by operating management and necessarily used to generate sales and operating profit viz:

fixed assets
plus *working capital* (i.e. stocks and work in progress plus trade debtors minus trade creditors). Ideally a minimum operating cash balance ought also to be included in working capital but it is not easy to isolate this element from that cash balance which merely represents a temporary surplus of funds; so for convenience cash and bank balances will be ignored when measuring working capital.

The total of fixed assets plus working capital will be referred to in this book as *Net Operating Assets* (to distinguish it from net *non*-operating assets).

cash flow:
— actual cash flow from operations, as defined on page 67.

Applying these rules to Typical Products Ltd. the following numbers emerge:

Last year £000s					This year £000s
2,025		Sales			3,500
123		Operating profit			168
		Net operating assets:			
	262	Fixed assets		430	
		Working capital			
	262	Stocks	703		
	254	Trade debtors	611		
	(201)	Trade creditors	(613)		
	315			701	
577					1,131
		Cash flow from operations			
103		(see page 208)			(386)

The reader is encouraged to ascertain the house rules for operating management performance appraisal adopted by his or her own company and compare them to those selected above.

Operating Profitability

Profitability must be the ultimate test of operating efficiency and often is the first financial ratio to look for when reading annual accounts. Notice that we are talking about profitability (indicating a ratio or the rate of earning profit) rather than the amount of profit itself.

Two operating profitability ratios can be calculated:

1. *Operating profit to sales*, i.e. operating profit for the year expressed as a percentage of sales for the year
2. *Operating profit to net operating assets*, i.e. operating profit for the year expressed as a percentage of the value, at the year end, of the resources employed to earn that operating profit. This ratio is variously referred to as return on investment (ROI), or return on capital employed (ROC) or, as we shall refer to it henceforth, *return on net operating assets*, or *RONA*.

The first ratio becomes more meaningful if an analysis of operating expenses is available and the ratio of each class of expense to sales is also calculated. Any changes in these latter ratios will indicate reasons for any variation in the operating profit to sales ratio. But RONA is the more important ratio of the two; one of the objects of making an investment is to earn a reasonable return: if the return obtained from an investment in net operating assets is inadequate, the investment perhaps might better be made elsewhere.

These two operating profitability ratios are closely related via a third ratio: the *asset turnover ratio*, or *velocity ratio*. This ratio reveals what sales have been generated for every £ invested in net operating assets and hence is the starting point for the measurement of asset productivity. Consider the following example:

	Company A	Company B
Sales	£1,000	£500
Operating profit	£100	£40
Net operating assets	£1,000	£250
Operating profit to sales	10%	8%
Velocity ratio, or asset turnover ratio (i.e. sales ÷ net operating assets)	1	2
RONA	10%	16%

Observe that company A turned over its net operating assets in sales only once but company B did it twice. Put another way: for every £1 of sales, company A required £1 of net operating assets whereas company B required only 50p. Here we have a compounding element in the operating profitability ratios: company A earned 10 percent on sales but earned this only once to produce 10 percent RONA whereas company B earned only 8 percent on sales but earned this twice to produce 16 percent RONA—a much better profitability performance than A. Notice therefore that when measuring RONA it is important to isolate its two compounding elements: operating profit to sales ratio and velocity ratio, and that the relationship between these two elements can be expressed in the following formula:

$$\text{RONA i.e. } \frac{\text{Operating profit}}{\text{Net operating assets}} = \frac{\text{Operating profit}}{\text{Sales}} \times \frac{\text{Sales}}{\underset{\uparrow}{\text{Net operating assets}}}$$

$$\text{Velocity ratio}$$

It therefore follows that there are two quite distinct routes to the improvement of operating profitability

— the one is concerned with cost control, pricing, sales volumes and sales mix; i.e. selling more profitably:
   which culminates in the ratio of operating profit to sales
— the other is concerned with fixed asset utilization, stock control and credit control; i.e. generating more sales from the same investment in net operating assets or reducing net operating assets for the same level of sales:
   which culminates in the velocity ratio.

And finally, do remember that the velocity ratio is a *multiplier*. In supermarket retailing of foods, for example, competition forces down the operating profit to sales ratio to very low levels so an adequate RONA can only be guaranteed by high velocity ratios; however in speculative house building or heavy engineering, where a high velocity ratio is difficult to achieve, it is much more important to generate a high operating profit to sales ratio if an adequate RONA is to be guaranteed.

Shareholder Profitability

We have seen that return on investment is the prime measure of profitability and that, in the case of operating management, return on investment is refined as RONA (operating profit expressed as a percentage of net operating assets).

But what of the shareholder? They would measure return on investment quite differently because they are primarily concerned with what's left in it for them, i.e. what is *their* return on *their* investment:

—the shareholders' profit is profit attributable to ordinary shareholders
—the shareholders' investment is shareholders' funds or equity interest
    (i.e. called up share capital plus the accumulation of reserves)

So the shareholders' return on investment is refined as profit attributable to ordinary shareholders for the year expressed as a percentage of shareholders' funds at the year end. We shall henceforth refer to this as *return on shareholders' funds* after tax, or ROSF (an alternative expression would be return on equity or ROE).

A shareholder may also wish to highlight how much the ROSF has been affected by corporation tax so, for comparison purposes, one may also calculate the profit before taxation for the year as a percentage of shareholders' funds at the year end.

Finally, instead of calculating ROSF (which is the profit attributable expressed as a percentage of shareholders' funds), a shareholder might calculate *EPS*—or *Earnings per Share* (which is the profit attributable divided by the number of ordinary shares).

To summarize: shareholder profitability is measured either in terms of:

    ROSF (ROE)
        —both before and after tax
or EPS
        —normally after tax only

both these would normally ignore extraordinary items. Their relationship to RONA is explained by capital gearing, which we must turn to next.

Capital Gearing (The Debt/Equity Ratio)

Capital gearing (sometimes called leverage) is simply a reflection of the mix of borrowed money (debt) to shareholders' money (equity) in the financing of a company. The higher the proportion borrowed, the higher is said to be the gearing; the lower the proportion borrowed, the lower the gearing.

Gearing is important to the shareholder because if money can be borrowed at a cost of interest lower than the RONA that can be earned by investing that money in net operating assets, the shareholder will benefit from the excess of RONA over the cost of interest as demonstrated in situation 1 below:

	Situation 1		Situation 2	
	A	B	A	B
Debt (i.e. borrowing) @ 10%	200	800	200	800
Equity (i.e. shareholders' funds)	800	200	800	200
Net operating assets	£1,000	£1,000	£1,000	£1,000
Operating profit	200	200	160	160
Interest on debt @ 10%	20	80	20	80
Profit before taxation	£180	£120	£140	£80
RONA (operating profit % net operating assets)	20%	20%	16%	16%
ROSF before tax (profit before taxation % shareholders' funds)	22.5%	60%	17.5%	40%

Notice that although firms A and B are both earning the same 20 percent RONA, the shareholder in B earns a higher before tax ROSF than the shareholder in A; moreover both sets of shareholders earn a higher before tax ROSF than has been generated from RONA. Such is the benefit of gearing to the shareholder: provided that RONA (20 percent) is higher than the cost of borrowing (10 percent), the higher the gearing the higher will be the before tax ROSF.

But of course what goes up might come down: the higher the gearing, the higher the volatility of ROSF and the greater the risk of a negative ROSF despite a small positive RONA. Consider a 20 percent decline in operating profit in the above demonstration, situation 2: notice that RONA declines by 20 percent also to 16 percent; ROSF in A falls by a little more than 20 percent to 17.5 percent; but ROSF in B falls by 33 percent from 60 percent to 40 percent.

The reader is invited to work out that if operating profit were to fall to £80, RONA would fall to 8 percent, ROSF in A would be 7.5 percent, but ROSF in B would be nil.

The *debt/equity ratio* simply reflects the degree of gearing: the higher the ratio the higher the gearing. Unfortunately two methods of measuring debt/equity are employed in practice so the reader is urged always to confirm which method has been used. The demonstration on page 96 revealed the following financial structure:

	A	B
Debt	200	800
Equity	800	200
Total financing	£1,000	£1,000

The most frequently used measure of debt/equity simply expresses debt as a percent of equity: 25 percent for A, 400 percent for B. But occasionally debt is expressed as a percent of total financing; 20 percent for A, 80 percent for B. Henceforth in this book we shall use the former basis of measurement rather than the latter.

A further variation in the computation of the debt/equity ratio in practice is whether it is based on *gross* debt (i.e. the total borrowings) or on the *net* debt (i.e. the total borrowings minus any positive cash or bank balances). This is demonstrated on page 102.

Having had that lengthy, but necessary, excursion into the principles of profitability analysis, let us return to the annual accounts of Typical Products Ltd. at Appendix B and see what they tell us about its financial performance. Note that £ references are in £000s through the rest of this chapter.

Operating Efficiency

Just how efficiently has operating management of Typical Products Ltd. performed over the last 2 years? Let us extract the relevant financial ratios.

(a) *Operating Profitability*

		Last year	This year	% change
Sales	a	£2,025	£3,500	+73%
Operating profit	b	£123	£168	+37%
Net operating assets (p. 92)	c	£577	£1,131	+96%
Operating profit to sales	b%a	6.1%	4.8%	
Velocity ratio	a÷c	3.5×	3.1×	
RONA	b%c	21.3%	14.9%	

These ratios reveal that, although operating profit has increased in amount, profitability has declined. Operating profit to sales is much lower this year than last—there is insufficient information to give any explanation for this.

But worse, the velocity ratio has also slowed down thus compounding the 1.3 points decline in operating profit to sales into a 6.4 points decline in RONA. Some explanation for the decline in velocity ratio will be revealed by subsequent ratios.

(b) *Asset Productivity*

		Last year	This year	% change
Stocks	a	262	703	+ 168%
Trade debtors	b	254	611	+ 141%
Trade Creditors	c	(201)	(613)	+ 205%
Working capital	d = a + b − c	315	701	+ 123%
Fixed assets	e	262	430	+ 64%
Net operating assets	f = d + e	£577	£1,131	+ 96%

In the light of the 73 percent increase in sales, there appears to have been an improvement in productivity of fixed assets but a decline in productivity of working capital.

Productivity in the three elements of working capital is often measured by the following further ratios:

1. *Stock turnover ratio*, which is an indicator of the number of times stock is replenished in a year, or how long it is held without moving.
2. *Debtors to sales ratio*, which is an indicator of the length of time it takes to collect from trade debtors, i.e. the average debtor collection period.
3. *Creditors to purchases ratio*, which is an indicator of the length of time being taken to pay trade creditors, i.e. the average creditor payment period.

These three ratios are discussed in greater detail in Chapter 13 but in the simplest form are calculated thus:

1. Strictly the stock turnover ratio should be calculated separately for raw materials, work in progress and finished goods by comparing average stock-holding at cost with usage at cost. Whilst this measure would be applied internally where cost of usage is available, this information is not always available in published accounts (and is not available for Typical Products Ltd.). As an alternative, some indication of the trend in stock turnover can be obtained by comparing stock with sales and expressing the answer either as a multiplier or as a percentage. This is meaningless insofar as it is comparing an item at cost with an item at selling price, but the trend of this

ratio will indicate any changes in velocity of stock turnover (unfortunately, changes in pricing policy will also affect the ratio calculated thus).

		Last year	This year
Sales	a	£2,025	£3,500
Stocks	b	£262	£703
Stock turnover *indicator:*	a ÷ b	7·7×	5×
	or b%a	12.9%	20%

The ratio indicates a slowing down in velocity of stock turnover.

2. Correct computation of the average debtor collection period from published accounts can be complex because:
   i. it is only credit sales to which debtors relate but the figure for sales in the profit and loss account includes both cash and credit sales
   ii sales in the profit and loss account excludes VAT, sales tax and excise but debtors in the balance sheet includes these items.

For these reasons a simple percentage of trade debtors to sales is often calculated because the trend in this percentage will indicate any changes in collection period.

		Last year	This year
Sales	a	£2,025	£3,500
Sales including VAT (assuming VAT @ 17½ %)	$b = a \times 117\frac{1}{2}\%$	£2,379	£4,113
Average daily sales	c = b ÷ 365	£6.5	£11.3
Trade debtors	d	£254	£611
Average collection period (assuming no cash sales)	e = d ÷ c	39 days	54 days
Trade debtors % sales	f = d%a	12.5%	17.5%

The ratios indicate an extension of the average debtor collection period.

3. Information on purchases would be available internally but it is not given in the published accounts of Typical Products Ltd. Therefore it is not possible to compute this ratio. However, as a general indicator of credit taken from suppliers, a simple percentage of trade creditors to sales can be calculated.

		Last year	This year
Sales	a	£2,025	£3,500
Trade creditors	b	£201	£613
Trade creditors % sales	c = b%a	9.9%	17.5%

The ratio indicates a considerable extension of credit taken from suppliers.

(c) *Cash Flow*

The cash flow statement on page 208 tells all: a £103 positive actual cash flow from operations last year can be compared to a negative £386 this year. The necessary investment in fixed assets of £229 this year to cope with the growth in sales was itself significant but by far the greatest negative influence was the declining productivity in working capital which caused a cash outflow of £386.

The three working capital productivity ratios which we have calculated above should have given rise to concern; the cash flow analysis puts a size to this concern: potential cash flow from operations this year amounted to £206 and, out of that, £441 was invested in additional stocks, £357 in longer collection period from trade debtors whilst extension of trade creditors generated £412.

Liquidity

A vital issue is the ability of a business to meet its obligations when they fall due. This leads to a comparison of current liabilities (the obligations) with current assets (out of which the obligations must be met) and to a consideration of the margin of safety between the two, i.e. the net current assets. The *current ratio*, measures this margin of safety by calculating the number of times the current assets cover the current liabilities:

		Last year	This year
Current assets	a	£538	£1,322
Current liabilities	b	£221	£847
Current ratio	a ÷ b	2·4 : 1	1·6 : 1

The ratio reveals that current liabilities are not as well covered this year as last: i.e. that the company is less able to meet its obligations when they fall due. This observation is consistent with our comment above on extension of trade creditors.

If all those to whom we owe money demanded payment now, could we quickly lay our hands on sufficient cash? This is the acid test of liquidity. Not all the current assets can be converted into cash quickly; in particular, stock may first have to be processed and then become a debtor before conversion into cash. The *acid test*, or *quick ratio*, measures the ability to pay by comparing current liabilities with quick assets (i.e. those which can quickly be converted into cash, generally taken as current assets minus stock):

		Last year	This year
Quick assets	a	£276	£619
Current liabilities	b	£221	£847
Acid test	a ÷ b	1·2 : 1	0·7 : 1

The ratio reveals the deterioration of the liquid position; in an emergency Typical Products Ltd. cannot meet all its obligations this year.

In computing the quick ratio one could argue that the bank overdraft should be excluded from the figure for current liabilities, as it might not normally have to be settled "quickly". If this were done the quick ratio this year would be 0·9 (i.e. £619, compared with £657): still a deterioration on last year.

Because the inclusion of the bank overdraft brings down this ratio from an almost acceptable 0·9 to an unacceptable 0·7 it does underline the danger of the overdraft's being recalled quickly. This firm must keep friends with the bank manager!

Overtrading

A common cause of deterioration of the liquid position is this killer disease of many a promising credit trading enterprise. Reduced to its simplest terms, overtrading is an expansion of sales with inadequate capital support. In order to expand, stocks and work in progress are built up and financed by increased demands on creditors, or by borrowing. Debtors also increase and there is a time lag before cash flows back to pay the creditors. There is an urge to borrow more or to offer cut prices for prompt cash; either way leads to reduced profits and irate creditors. This was also touched upon in Chapter 8.

The danger of overtrading also underlines the importance of the three working capial productivity ratios introduced at page 98.

1. Stock turnover ratio
2. Debtors to sales ratio
3. Creditors to purchases ratio

Working capital management is taken further in Chapter 13.

Financial Structure

We have seen that declining productivity of working capital in Typical Products Ltd. has led to a negative cash flow from operations which in turn has led to declining liquidity ratios and recourse to increased borrowing. What has this done to the financial structure of the company and how safe is the borrowing? Let us dig out some more numbers from page 207:

		Last year	This year
12% Debentures	a	50	50
Bank overdraft	b	—	190
Total (or gross) debt	c = a + b	50	240
Cash at bank and in hand	d	22	8
Net debt	e = c − d	£28	£232
Equity (i.e. shareholders' funds)	f	£490	£809
Gross debt/equity ratio	g = c%f	10.2%	29.7%
Net debt/equity ratio	h = e%f	5.7%	28.7%

This is a considerable increase in gearing but does not necessarily represent a level which the company cannot live with.

An additional measure of borrowing safety is the *interest cover*: this indicates by how much operating profit can fall before it ceases to provide for interest. Inability to meet the interest payment is bad news for the lender!

		Last year	This year
Operating profit	a	£123	£168
Interest payable	b	£6	£26
Interest cover	c = a ÷ b	20.5 ×	6.5 ×

The declining interest cover would certainly be looked upon with disfavour by the lending banker.

In the same way that some analysts calculate the debt/equity ratio on the gross basis and some on the net basis, so interest cover might be calculated on a gross or net basis as demonstrated below:

Operating profit	a	100
Interest received	b	10
Interest payable	c	30
Gross interest cover	d = (a + b) ÷ c	110 ÷ 30 = 3.7 ×
Net interest cover	e = a ÷ (c − b)	100 ÷ 20 = 5.0 ×

Shareholder Satisfaction

How happy is the shareholder of Typical Products Ltd. going to be? Let us do some more ratios on the lines described on pages 95 to 97.

(a) *Shareholder Profitability*

We have seen that RONA has declined and that the debt/equity ratio has increased. What is the combined impact of these on ROSF and EPS?

		Last year	This year
Profit attributable to Typical Products Ltd. shareholders	a	£65	£82
Shareholders' funds	b	£490	£809
Number of ordinary shares	c	250	450
ROSF after tax	d = a%b	13.2%	10.1%
EPS	e = a ÷ c	26.0p	18.2p

ROSF after tax has also declined but not quite as steeply as RONA; the shareholder has been shielded somewhat by the combined impact of higher gearing and lower tax charge as the following further ratios demonstrate:

		Last year	This year
Profit before taxation	a	£117	£142
Total capital and reserves	b	£498	£817
Corporation tax charge	c	£51	£58
ROSF before tax	d = a%b	23.5%	17.4%
RONA (see page 97)	e	21.3%	14.9%
Benefit from gearing	f = d − e	+ 1.9%	+ 2.5%
Rate at which corporation tax suffered	g = c%a	43.6%	40.8%

So shareholder profitability is not as bad as it might have been; but the shareholders will no doubt be less than enthusiastic about this performance, particularly bearing in mind that they have been asked to invest £300 more capital in the company via the rights issue this year.

(b) *Dividend*

One of the objects of making an investment is to receive a satisfactory rate of return in cash; in the case of a share, this is provided by the dividend. The rate of dividend is of course important: from Typical Products Ltd. the ordinary dividend went up from 11p per share last year (4p interim plus 7p final) to 13.2p per share this year (4.4p interim plus 8.8p final). An equally important matter is the *dividend cover*, which indicates what proportion of the profit for the year has actually been distributed in dividend (as opposed to being transferred to reserves). Dividend cover thus indicates on the one hand the margin of safety, or the amount by which profit for the year can be allowed to fall before the dividend might be reduced. On the other hand it indicates the proportion of profit attributable which has been transferred to reserves (i.e. reinvested in the company to cover inflation or to provide for future growth): the greater the dividend cover the greater the reinvestment, and vice versa. For Typical Products Ltd., it is:

		Last year	This year
Profit attributable to Typical Products Ltd. shareholders	a	£65	£82
Profit for the financial year	b	£62	£79
Dividends	c	£28	£60
Dividend cover before extra-ordinary items	$d = a \div c$	2.3 times	1.4 times
Dividend cover after extra-ordinary items	$e = b \div c$	2.2 times	1.3 times

The ratio reveals a considerable reduction in reinvestment and in margin of safety for the ordinary dividend which will no doubt add to the shareholders' lack of enthusiasm. In theory of course the rate of dividend can be maintained by drawing from the accumulated reserves: however it is most unlikely that these reserves will be represented by actual cash so they should not be relied upon too strongly as a potential source of cash dividend.

In addition to the cover, each shareholder is also interested in the *yield* he is obtaining on his investment. Yield is calculated by expressing his annual income as a percentage of his capital invested. For example, the additional £1 ordinary shares issued by Typical Products Ltd. this year were issued at £1.50 (notice that there is an increase of £200 in called up share capital but also £100 in share premium, indicating an issue at a premium of 50p). If I bought 100 shares (nominal value £100) they would have cost me £150 and my yield would be calculated as follows:

Nominal value of investment in 100 shares	a	£100
Dividend thereon @ 13.2p	b	£13.2
Actual cost of investment	c	£150
Actual yield	$b \div c$	8.8%

Other than an initial purchase of shares from the company, each shareholder will no doubt buy shares at a different price depending on the prevailing market price of the share at the date of purchase. Therefore in practice dividend yield is a calculation which is personal to each shareholder. Yields which are quoted in the financial press are normally calculated by reference to the closing market price on the day to which the quote relates.

(c) *Share Value*

What is a share worth? A similar question was posed on page 35, "What is a business worth?", and the answer is the same: "Whatever a willing buyer is prepared to pay". Shares in a public company have an advantage here, because a ready market is provided in the Stock Exchange, whose official quotation provides a basis of value for a particular share transaction. But what of a private company? Share valuation here must be something for negotiation and a starting figure often selected is the *net book value* of the share. This is simply the net assets attributable to shareholders divided by the number of shares issued.

Net assets attributable to ordinary shareholders of Typical Products Ltd. can be computed from the balance sheet by taking total net assets and deducting therefrom the proportion attributable to other than ordinary shareholders (i.e. minority interests in subsidiaries). A more direct way of getting the same answer is simply pick up the figure for shareholders' funds. Net book value of an ordinary share is therefore:

		Last year	This year
Shareholders' funds (i.e. Net assets attributable to ordinary shareholders)	a	£490	£809
Number of ordinary shares issued	b	250	450
Net book value of one ordinary share	a ÷ b	£1.96	£1.80

The theory behind this valuation is that if the company were to close down at the balance-sheet date, realize all the assets *at their balance-sheet values* and pay off all the liabilities and prior charges—there would be left, in cash, for each holder of a £1 ordinary share £1.96 last year and £1.80 this year. This is why the net book value of a share is often referred to as the share's *break-up value*. Many people, including some investment analysts, set great store by break-up value, but a brief recap of those sections of Chapter 4 relating to goodwill and asset valuation will put this value in its true perspective. A balance sheet does not reflect the true commercial value of a business, similarly a balance sheet value of a share cannot reflect the true commercial value of that share. As stated earlier, the net book calculation is only a starting figure in the negotiation for a sale; a valuation based on future earnings is often computed, on a similar basis to the method of valuing goodwill outlined on page 37. ("Future earnings" would be total profit attributable to shareholders if all the shares were being sold, but perhaps dividend only if a minority shareholding only were being sold.)

The *price earnings ratio* (*P/E ratio*) is widely used as an indicator of share value. This, as the name implies, is simply a comparison of market price with earnings per share. On the assumption that the buyer of a share is buying a proportion of the future earnings, the higher the P/E ratio the more highly is the share valued by the market. It is interesting to compare the P/E ratio of one share with another within the same industry, (referred to as a share's *P/E relative*). Assuming the market price of an ordinary share in Typical Products Ltd. is 154·7 its P/E ratio on this year's earnings is calculated thus:

Profit attributable to Typical Products Ltd. shareholders	a	£82
Number of ordinary shares issued	b	450
EPS	c = a ÷ b	18·2p
Assumed market price	d	154·7
P/E ratio	d ÷ c	8·5

and if similar shares enjoy a P/E ratio of 14·2, then Typical Products P/E relative is 8·5% 14·2 or 60%.

There can be no simple formula for valuing a share because it is so much a personal matter between the seller and an individual willing buyer. As was the case with valuing goodwill: "How badly do you want it—how much are you willing to pay?"

Desirable Ratios

The reader may ask, "What is a desirable ratio?" or, "Is the ratio I have calculated good or bad?" It is difficult to answer these questions because much depends upon the nature of business carried on, the stage of development reached and the general economic situation. However, some general comments are appropriate:

1. *Operating efficiency*

An adequate level of RONA should reward the business risks undertaken and also cover the cost of capital which has been raised to finance the net operating assets. What is desirable will therefore be affected by prevailing interest rates and shareholder expectations, business risks, inflation and taxation; under the conditions prevailing at the time of writing it would seem that, in the U.K., 20 percent to 25 percent in historical cost terms should be a minimum acceptable RONA.

Within this RONA the combination of operating profit to sales and velocity ratios depends very much on the nature of the business and any combination from a high operating profit to sales/low velocity ratio (more typical of say heavy engineering) to a low operating profit to sales/high velocity ratio (more typical of say supermarket food retailing) is possible as demonstrated by the following graph:

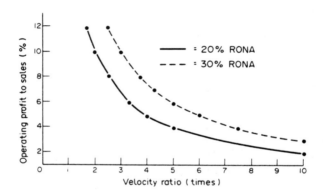

Desirable ratios for stock turn and credit collection periods clearly depend upon individual business environments, credit terms etc.

Cash flow from operations ideally ought to be sufficiently positive to permit a degree of internal growth without constant recourse to external financing. However some products are inherently cash consumers (consider the continuing investment which is demanded by stocks of maturing scotch whisky, for example) whilst some are inherently cash generators (consider a supermarket for example which sells quickly for cash and pays slowly on credit). This aspect of operations presents an interesting problem of strategic business mix to many organizations.

2. *Liquidity*

A widely held view is that the current ratio should be at least 2:1, indeed it has been referred to as the "two to one ratio". This is misleading because different business environments may require more or less than this. However, it is not unreasonable to expect at least 1:1 in the acid test ratio.

3. *Financial structure*

What is a desirable debt/equity ratio for any company depends very much upon the risk preference of the board of directors ... but in the ultimate no company can borrow more than the lender is prepared to lend! At the time of writing debt/equity ratios in the U.K. and the U.S.A. tend not to go beyond 50 percent to 60 percent but in the rest of Western Europe they tend to be somewhat higher whilst in Australia and the Far East they tend to be considerably higher.

Interest cover ought to be quite high for safety and a multiple of between 5 and 10 would not be considered excessive.

4. *Shareholder Satisfaction*

Acceptable dividends, dividend growth, dividend cover, dividend yield, EPS and P/E ratios can only be determined by comparison with other investment opportunities. The *Financial Times* or similar publication provides such a basis of comparison on a daily basis within classified industrial grouping. Brokers and other institutions also provide share information services.

Typical Products Ltd. Review

We have now read the published accounts of Typical Products Ltd.; what story have they told?

Beginning with the Profit and Loss Account, we see that sales of the Group increased by 73 percent from £2025 last year to £3500 this year but that operating profit increased by only 37 percent from £123 last year to £168 this year. Of this £168, interest absorbed £26, taxation £58 and, £2 belonged to minority interests in subsidiaries. This left £82 attributable to shareholders, an increase of £17 on last year; out of this a dividend of 13·2p on the ordinary shares is proposed, compared with 11p last year. The balance of profits, £19 this year against £34 last year, goes to swell reserves, i.e. is "ploughed back" to cover the impact of inflation and to provide for growth.

So far as operations are concerned, the year has seen a tremendous increase in sales but this was achieved at lower margins. This expansion must have required additional capital and the increased charge for depreciation (£38 against £13) indicates substantial acquisitions of assets. The balance sheet will indicate the source of this necessary additional finance.

The proportion of profits distributed as dividend has increased (i.e. the dividend cover has been reduced)—the rate of ordinary dividend was increased despite the reduction in profitability. This may indicate a more liberal dividend policy on the part of the directors, who perhaps feel that it is no longer necessary to plough back such a large proportion of profits for expansion purposes.

Turning to the Balance Sheet we notice signs of the expansion which has taken place. Net operating assets have increased by 96% from £577 to £1131 but it is interesting to note that tangible fixed assets account for only £168 of the increase; additional stock of £441 and debtors of £357 were also necessary to help promote the expansion. This position is confirmed by the Cash Flow Statement, which also reminds us that the necessary finance comes mainly from three sources:

1. Additional credit was obtained from suppliers—£412.
2. Additional £1 shares were issued at £1.50, producing £300.
3. The balance at bank was run down and overdraft facilities of £190 were created.

One wonders whether the £300 from additional shares was sufficient because the liquid position is now under severe strain, the quick ratio being less than unity. Furthermore, the owners have now less than 50 percent financial stake in the business, creditors and bank overdraft are providing almost the same amount between them. It would appear that the company would be in a healthier position if more permanent capital were available. However, if the future profits are expected to be much higher than this year, the directors may be hoping to reduce the reliance upon bank and creditors by using future ploughed-back profits as a source of finance—yet this is hardly borne out by the current dividend policy.

Net operating assets, at their enhanced amount this year, have not been employed as efficiently as last year; the main reason for this is the disproportionate increase in amount of stock and debtors. The rate of turnover of stock has slowed down whilst the average collection period for debtors has increased—both unwelcome trends. (But beware: in this case the trend in these two measures may be misleading: much depends on when the sales expansion took place. If the expansion got under way late in the year, stock and debtors at the year end are clearly representative of a higher *annual rate* of sales than this year's total sales of £3500. The comparison undertaken for this year on pages 98–99 would then be invalid until an *annual rate of sales* were substituted for the actual sales figure.)

To sum up ... Typical Products Ltd. has expanded rapidly, almost doubling its sales within 12 months, and to finance this expansion, £300 was raised from shareholders. Substantial acquisition of property and plant was made but the increased level of activity also demanded increased working capital. Perhaps the £300 was insufficient because the liquid position is now under severe strain and recourse has been made to the bank for substantial overdraft facilities. Profitability at the new level of activity is lower than at the old, and although the ordinary dividend has been increased slightly, the cover is reduced.

This very brief financial appraisal relates the more obvious points revealed by the figures contained in this set of published accounts which have been produced on the historical cost convention and therefore ignore inflation. However, a financial appraisal can be only one of the many pieces of information required to make a decision on this company. Other necessary information would include details of the expansion which has taken place, the nature of the company's business activities, its future prospects and the calibre of its management. These and other vital pieces of non-financial information must be obtained before the picture of Typical Products Ltd. is complete.

But Beware ...

The final word on the subject must be one of repeated caution. All the ratios which have been used as the basis for our financial evaluation of Typical Products Ltd. have been calculated from the balance sheet and profit and loss account. Two observations are relevant:

1. The balance sheet represents the financial position at the year end (and may have been carefully "window dressed" for the occasion). What did it look like on the other 364 days in the year and could this have coloured our views?

2. Does the profit and loss account represent a normal year and is it reasonable to assume that the figures accumulated at a steady rate throughout the year? The large piece in parenthesis towards the top of p. 110 (But beware: . . .) is worth reiterating in the case of Typical Products Ltd. which has had a most unusual year of growth.

CHAPTER 12

Structured Use of Financial Ratios

IN THE preceding chapter we reviewed some of the financial ratios which could be calculated for Typical Products Ltd. and several times made reference to the possibility of calculating more had more data been available. How many ratios do you need and how can you pick your way through them? This is the topic to which we address our attention in this chapter.

Interrelationship Between Ratios

Financial ratio analysis aims to provide a useful, if sometimes rough, analytical tool which can be used for diagnosis, planning and control of business performance. But eventually a considerable number of ratios could be computed and tabulated thereby creating for the reader a real danger of utter confusion. The way to overcome this is to look for cause and effect relationships between ratios: in this way it is possible to pick a route through ratios in a logical progression which follows orders of priorities or chains of events.

A good example of interrelationship and progression was developed between pages 93 and 94 where we observed an interrelationship between three ratios as follows:

$$\text{RONA i.e.} \quad \frac{\text{Operating profit}}{\text{Net operating assets}} = \frac{\text{Operating profit}}{\text{Sales}} \times \frac{\text{Sales}}{\text{Net operating assets}}$$

The first ratio is a compound of the other two; therefore changes in the first would be explained by changes in the other two. Similarly if we now wished to explain changes in the operating profit to sales ratio we would look for a small number of major income/expenditure ratios, each of which would then be explained by a further sequence of ratios and so on. Similarly changes in the third ratio above would be explained by a sequence of asset productivity ratios again following a logical progression of cause and effect relationship.

Pyramid Presentation

This logical progression is aided by the manner in which ratios are presented. A useful schematic concept is to think of ratios in the form of a pyramid structure or "fault-finding chart". The fault-finding pyramid concept is used in many technical situations where it is necessary to get to the root of a problem quickly; examples are in the control of a piece of process plant or the operation of a motor car: if the thing does not work correctly it is sensible to progress through a logical sequence of interrelated cause-and-effect steps until the trouble spot is located.

Applying this concept to financial ratio analysis we could begin a pyramid with the three ratios referred to above as follows:

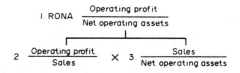

Because there are only two types of net operating assets, namely fixed assets and working capital, ratio 3 is explained as follows:

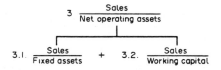

and ratio 3·2 is obviously explained by the stock turnover ratio, the debtors to sales ratio and the creditors to purchases ratio because stocks, debtors and creditors are the three elements of working capital.

Eventually the whole thing can be put together into one pyramid, each successive line of which explains the movement in the line above. An example of such a completed pyramid appears on page 115. Some of the expressions used there below ratio 2 will not be explained until Chapter 15 but are included at this stage for completeness.

Variations on the Theme

The pyramid on page 115 is an example only of the concept, not necessarily the one possible method of presentation. In particular the following variations might appeal to the reader:

1. If it is felt that operating management is better measured against their use of total operating assets then this would appear as the denominator of ratios 1 and 3 instead of net operating assets. The denominator of 3·2 would then become current assets and ratio 3·2·3 would disappear.

2. Chapter 7 made the point that sales might not be a valid measure of activity. In this case the substitution of value added for sales throughout the pyramid might be more meaningful.

3. If the concept of a velocity, or turnover ratio is difficult to grasp, ratio 3 could be amended to reflect instead net operating assets as percent of sales; e.g. instead of saying that the sales to net operating assets ratio is 4, one would say that net operating assets are 25 percent of sales—and so on down the right-hand side of the pyramid on page 115.

4. The pyramid could be drafted to progress horizontally across the page instead of vertically down the page.

Application to Typical Products Ltd.

As a demonstration of this structured approach to financial ratio analysis, a financial fault finding chart for Typical Products Ltd., employing variation 3 above, appears on page 116 using the ratios developed in the previous chapter. Note how the decline in RONA is sequentially explained by successive lines on the chart: control of stocks and debtors eventually emerge as the chief culprits.

Pyramid of ratios revealing the financial performance of operating management

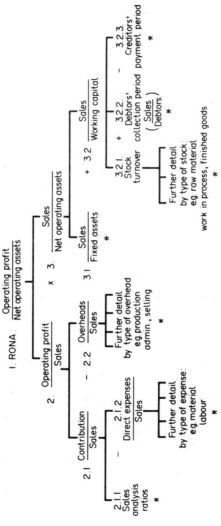

1. RONA: $\dfrac{\text{Operating profit}}{\text{Net operating assets}}$

2. $\dfrac{\text{Operating profit}}{\text{Sales}}$

$\times$ 3. $\dfrac{\text{Sales}}{\text{Net operating assets}}$

2.1 $\dfrac{\text{Contribution}}{\text{Sales}}$ − 2.2 $\dfrac{\text{Overheads}}{\text{Sales}}$

3.1 $\dfrac{\text{Sales}}{\text{Fixed assets}}$ * + 3.2 $\dfrac{\text{Sales}}{\text{Working capital}}$

2.1.1 Sales analysis ratios *

2.1.2 $\dfrac{\text{Direct expenses}}{\text{Sales}}$

Further detail by type of expense: eg. material labour *

Further detail by type of overhead eg. production admin., selling *

3.2.1 Stock turnover

3.2.2 Debtors' collection period $\left(\dfrac{\text{Sales}}{\text{Debtors}}\right)$ *

+ − 3.2.3 Creditors' payment period *

Further detail by type of stock: eg. raw material work in process, finished goods *

* Each leg could be further analysed to give necessary detail

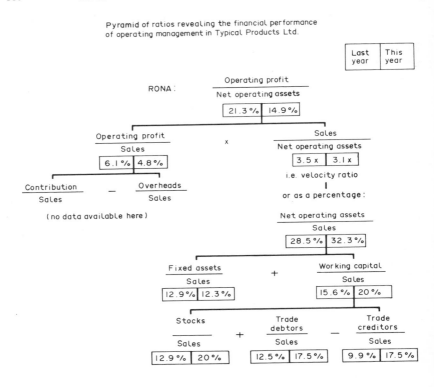

Pyramid of ratios revealing the financial performance of operating management in Typical Products Ltd.

Diagnosis; Planning; Control

Once the pyramid structure is grasped, it forms a useful framework not only for diagnosing financial troubles but also for planning and for control. For instance, if management wishes to improve RONA by 5 percent, what does this imply for all the ratios down the line; what are the interrelationships, the trade-offs, the practical possibilities? Similarly what are the most significant items to keep under close control down the pyramid to prevent a deterioration working its way to the top?

The concept also aids financial analysis via interdivision or interfirm comparison. If ratios between comparable units are compiled on a consistent basis and structured in the fault finding pyramid concept, much can be learned of the comparative strengths and weaknesses of each unit. A number of organizations offer such schemes of interfirm comparison; the major problem to be overcome is that of ensuring genuine comparability both between the basis of computation of the ratios used and between the firms being compared.

The last word on the subject must again be that financial ratio analysis should never be seen as an end in itself but only one aspect of that data which is necessary to guide a firm towards improved performance, growth and stability.

Shareholder Satisfaction

Thus far we have concentrated our attention on operating management's performance. The pyramid concept can be applied equally to ratios calculated in respect of shareholder satisfaction and the pyramid reproduced below is a simplified example of how this might be done. Notice that all ratios are ultimately interrelated because the top of the pyramid on page 115 slots into the bottom of the pyramid below.

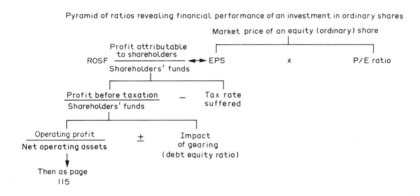

Pyramid of ratios revealing financial performance of an investment in ordinary shares

How Relevant is RONA?

RONA has been selected in this and the previous chapter as the basis for measuring, in financial terms, the performance of operating management; comments were made on page 91 regarding the importance of clearly defining this basis. But must it be RONA? Not necessarily—a measure will be selected which is relevant to the manner in which a particular business is conducted and to the nature of decisions which operating management can take to improve their financial performance. Alternatives which this author has met in practice are:

1. Comparable expressions to RONA; e.g. ROAM (Return on Assets Managed), ROTCE (Return on Trading Capital Employed), ROCA (Return on Controllable Assets)—but all these expressions were based on a definition of the investment in operating management which was essentially similar to the Net Operating Asset definition used in this book.

2. Because the balance sheet is true at one point in time only, it would be better to base the calculation on the average net operating assets employed throughout the accounting period rather than on those employed at the period end balance sheet date—hence ROANTA (Return on Average Net Trading Assets) and ROATCE (Return on Average Trading Capital Employed) and so on.

3. Point 1 on page 114 made reference to the use of ROTA—return on *total* operating assets rather than *net* operating assets.

4. Where operating management prefer a percentage of sales measure rather than a return on investment measure then Manageable Profit % Sales has been used alone instead of RONA. But in this case the definition of manageable profit is: operating profit minus a heavy internal finance charge based on the working capital employed by the operating manager concerned—this charge is thus a proxy for the velocity ratio which we have used in this book.

The whole concept of RONA, together with its variations, is particularly relevant to an *investment* driven business—but what about a *people* driven business (e.g. a consultancy or market research business). In this case the investment in net operating assets might be minuscule and RONA would be a misleadingly huge percentage. Perhaps here "ROPE" could be the answer!—Return on People Employed—and in such a case a pyramid of ratios could proceed as follows:

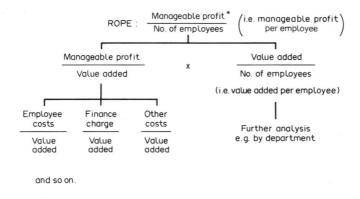

and so on.

*defined as opposite.

It is not RONA itself, it is the selection of a relevant measure and then following this through to individual operating manager actions using the cause and effect fault finding approach outlined in this chapter which brings benefits.

The final word must be one of caution. A business exists for the pursuit of *long-term* RONA. Beware the overbearing guidance of financial measures which reveal short-term improvements in RONA or its equivalent but which hide catastrophic consequences in the long term. Failure to invest in fixed assets; failure to pay creditors; failure to spend on product development, management development, marketing or preventative maintenance will all improve short-term RONA, but "aprés moi le deluge"!

Never use hard RONA information in isolation; always look at it alongside other, softer, non-financial information which will indicate the extent to which operating, or non-operating, managers are taking thought for the morrow.

CHAPTER 13

Management of Working Capital

WORKING capital was introduced at page 92. For simplicity in this book we have assumed that it consists of three elements only: stocks and work in progress plus trade debtors minus trade creditors. In certain circumstances (e.g. retail operations) a minimum operating cash balance might also be included. We have seen that working capital is the major item controllable by operating management down the right-hand side of the RONA pyramid, or fault-finding chart, introduced in Chapter 12. We also noted in Chapter 8 that the movement in working capital is a significant element in the determination of Cash Flow from Operations. Moreover, working capital is expensive to carry: costs are incurred in handling it, recording it, protecting it, financing it; the higher the working capital, the higher these costs and the lower the profit. Therefore, it seems appropriate at this stage to review in a little more detail some of the elements of working capital measurement, management and control.

How Much Working Capital is Required?

Working capital is essential to any business and we have noted above that it represents a significant element in both RONA and cash flow from operations. What would your RONA and cash flow from operations look like if there were no working capital? We computed RONA for Typical Products Ltd this year in Chapter 11:

$$\frac{\text{Operating profit}}{\text{Net operating assets}} \quad \frac{168}{1131} = 14.9\%.$$

Had there been no investment in working capital, RONA would have been $168/430 = 39.1$ percent. (In fact, RONA would have been even higher than that because operating profit would have been higher due to the elimination of costs associated with the carrying of working capital.) Similarly, without that large working capital movement, Typical Product's cash flow from opeations would not have been negative and interest would not have been incurred.

Clearly it is impossible to run a business with zero working capital; but what would your RONA and cash flow from operations look like if working capital were reduced by 5 percent, 10 percent and so on? It is good management practice to develop target levels for working capital linked to targets for RONA and cash flow from operations.

When fixing target levels it is important to remember that the size of working capital tends to move in sympathy with variations in volume: as volume increases, working capital increases and vice versa. Moreover, we have also seen in Chapter 9 that even when volume is static, the value of working capital will increase due to the impact of inflation.

To recap; the lower the working capital:

— the lower the net operating assets and hence the higher is RONA;
— the lower are the carrying costs and so the higher is the operating profit and hence the higher is RONA;
— the better is the cash flow from operations and so the lower is the need for borrowing and hence the lower is the interest which has to be paid.

In some businesses (e.g. supermarkets and some civil engineering contractors) it is normal to operate on a *negative* working capital (i.e. the trade creditors is in excess of the stocks and work in progress plus trade debtors). In such businesses it is necessary to maintain as high a negative as possible; this is equivalent to the need to maintain as low a positive working capital as possible in those businesses (e.g. manufacturing) which normally operate on a positive working capital.

So let us now look at the individual elements of working capital, remind ourselves of the way in which they are measured and review some steps which can be taken to ensure that a positive working capital is as low as possible or a negative working capital is as high as possible.

Measurement of Stocks and Work in Progress

The total of stocks and work in progress is made up of everything which has been bought or produced but has not yet been sold or consumed: so it includes raw material stocks, work in progress, sub-assemblies, finished goods, goods in transit and also stocks of fuel, machinery spares, drawing office supplies, stationery and so on. It might be the result of careful planning in order to balance the sequence of purchasing–production–sales or to minimize the risk of a stock out; on the other hand, it might be the result of bad planning, imbalance, duplication, scrap or obsolescence. The value can be significant, particularly in seasonal businesses where it becomes necessary deliberately to build up stock in anticipation of seasonal demand.

Stock turnover ratio is the basis for measuring how efficiently each component of stocks and work in progress is being managed. Stock turnover ratio was introduced at page 98 and the reader is invited to reread that section at this stage.

Because stocks are held to service the future rather than the past, stock turnover ratios should be computed in relation to estimated future usage. However, if this is not possible, the computation ought at least to be made by reference to recent rates of usage (e.g. the last quarter or the last month) rather than to usage over the whole past year, as was done on page 98. (The annualized method had to be adopted there in the absence of the degree of detail which would be available from an efficient internal management accounting routine.)

Wherever possible, stock turnover ratios should be based on a comparison of *quantities* of stocks used to quantities of stocks held rather than on a comparison of *values* of stocks used to values of stocks held. The golden rule must always be to compare like with like: if values are used, there is the danger that the basis of valuation of stock usage might differ from the basis of valuation of stocks held.

Management of Stocks and Work in Progress

A detailed review of the techniques of managing stocks and work in progress is beyond the scope of this book and the reader is invited to consult one of the many works of reference which specialize in stock management. However, a few practical pointers are noted below:

1. An efficient system of stock management will predetermine targets for key measures such as maximum, minimum and buffer stocks; re-order levels and order quantities; economic batch sizes; delivery frequencies and any other determinant of the size and duration of each of the components of stocks and work in progress.

2. The application of JIT (Just in Time) techniques have produced startling reductions in both stocks and work in progress, particularly when

they are applied, not only in the context of external supplier relationships, but also in the context of internal department-to-department movements of stocks and work in progress.

3. Efficient process planning will ensure that any movement of stocks through a production process will add value. Ideally, a piece should be picked up from the supplier, processed through to its finished state and handed over to the customer in one movement. An impossible ideal perhaps, but any additional movements picking up and putting down add *cost* but do not add *value* which delivers operating profit.

4. Significant reductions in stocks and work in progress levels have been achieved through the rationalization of parts and processes and the reduction in range of items carried.

5. Significant reductions have also been achieved by reducing the number of and/or size of physical stock locations. Human nature is such that it is easier to acquire and store, squirrel fashion, rather than to dispose of stock. The greater the number of stock locations or the greater the size of each container, the greater is the chance that each of these locations and containers will be filled. If there is nowhere to put it, stock cannot be carried — which after all is why JIT came about in the first place.

6. Above all, it is vital that ultimate responsibility for levels of stocks and work in progress should rest with a sufficiently senior manager. If responsibility for stock levels rests with, say, a relatively junior storeman who is "beaten over the head" every time there is a stock out, the odds are he will over-stock for safety; if levels of work in progress are left to the decision of a relatively junior departmental factory foreman, the odds are he will prefer to carry excess stocks and work in progress to ensure smooth production flow and a quiet life.

Measurement of Trade Debtors

Debtor collection period, or debtors-to-sales ratio, is the basis for measuring how efficiently trade debtors are being managed. This ratio was introduced at page 98 and the reader is invited to reread that section at this stage.

In the absence of more detailed information the calculation on page 99 was based on a daily sales figure averaged over the whole year; as such, it suffers from two serious weaknesses:

— the sales may not have occurred at an even rate throughout the year; if sales were proportionately higher towards the end of the year, then

reported debtor collection period calculated in this manner will be too high — and vice versa;
— the calculation averages out all credit customers, some of whom might pay promptly whilst others take a longer time to pay.

For these reasons the calculation of debtor collection period in practice, armed with the necessary degree of detail provided by an efficient financial accounting system, is carried out as follows:

1. An actual "countback" of sales invoiced is carried out. For example, the trade debtors of Typical Products Ltd. were £611 at the end of this year (let us assume this to be 31st December). If actal sales invoiced (including VAT, sales tax, excise and anything else which has been included in the debtors figure of £611) in the later months of the year had been:

December	(31 days)	£200
November	(30 days)	£100
October	(31 days)	£622
September	(30 days)	£400

then the debtors is made up of the following invoiced sales on a countback basis:

	Invoiced in the month		Running total	
All December's sales	31 days	£200	31 days	£200
All November's sales	30 days	£100	61 days	£300
Half of October's sales	15 days	£311	76 days	£611

i.e. the actual debtor collection period is some 76 days rather than the average of 54 days calculated on page 99.

2. This countback calculation is then supported by a schedule of "aged" debtors: e.g. what part of the £611 has been outstanding for 0 to 30 days, 31 to 60 days, 61 to 90 days, beyond 90 days. There would also be a detailed schedule of individual customers who were in the longest day categories.

Two further calculations could usefully be carried out to reveal how significant debtor collection is to an individual firm:

— How many days can a debt be outstanding before the profit on the sale is eliminated by the cost of interest on the cash borrowed to finance the outstanding debt? Clearly, the narrower the profit margin the quicker the profit will be eroded, as the following table demonstrates:

Profit margin (% sales)	Cost of bank borrowing (% p.a.)		
	10	14	18
	Number of days to erode profit		
1	36	26	20
2	72	51	39
5	180	129	99

— What additional good sales have to be generated to pay for each £1 of bad debt?

Management of Trade Debtors

Extended credit is an accepted part of business trading and may be an essential element of a firm's sales/marketing strategy. On the other hand, extended credit increases financial risk if the debtor does not pay. Clearly, therefore, it might not be possible to eliminate debtors altogether, but it certainly is necessary to manage them down to their lowest level consistent with sales/marketing strategy, so reducing both the level of working capital and the financial risk to the firm.

Efficient management of trade debtors has the following three aspects:

1. Clearly defined responsibility for credit management at a sufficiently senior management level in the firm. The scope of professional credit management will embrace:

(a) assessment of creditworthiness of potential new customers;
(b) monitoring the creditworthiness of existing customers;
(c) establishing, agreeing with customers and enforcing credit limits;
(d) arranging insurance if necessary (particularly in respect of export sales);
(e) prompt pursuit of slow payers.

2. An efficient financial accounting system which ensures that any delay in settlement is only attributable to the debtor and not to our own shortcomings, for example:

— prompt invoicing and rendering of statements;
— prompt handling of invoice queries raised by debtors;
— prompt banking of monies received;

— frequent reporing of debtor collection periods (as outlined in the previous section, page 124) and of individual customer performance against credit limits.

3. Knowledge of the payment procedures of major customers, e.g.:

— Does the customer "close the books" on one day in the month to begin a supplier payment routine: if so, what is that day? If we get our invoice into the customer's system on the day following closure, *we* will have added 30 days to the settlement period, not the customer.
— Who signs the cheques, i.e. who should we speak to if payment has not been received? It is unlikely to be the person who placed the order with our sales department.

Cash discounts are sometimes offered as an inducement to early settlement by the customer. If so, the system for the management of trade debtors should also ensure:

(a) That evaluation of the financial impact of discounts is correctly performed. This is best done by converting the discount into an equivalent percentage rate per annum: for example, to offer $2^1/_2$ percent discount for settlement in 10 days instead of normal 30-day terms is to offer $2^1/_2$ percent for accelerating the payment by 20 days which is equivalent to:

$$2^1/_2 \times \frac{365}{20} = 46 \text{ percent per annum.}$$

Surely there must be a cheaper alternative source of finance!

(b) That the offer is adequately monitored to prevent the customer taking both the discount and the credit.

Factoring is a means of passing the responsibility for administration and collection of debtors to a third party, generally a specialized finance house. For a fee, the factor advances cash to a firm "up front" in exchange for sales invoices and then assumes responsibility for subsequent collection of the debt on behalf of the firm. The fee is normally higher than bank overdraft rate, but it must be remembered that the factor is providing administrative services on behalf of the firm in addition to providing finance. Do note, however, that a factor does not normally take on the risk of bad debt: if the customer does not pay, the amount is charged back to the firm who raised the invoice, whose responsibility it then is to attempt to collect the outstanding debt.

Measurement of Trade Creditors

Creditor payment period, or creditors-to-purchases ratio, is the basis for measuring how efficiently trade creditors are being managed. This ratio was introduced at pages 98/99 and the reader is invited to reread these sections at this stage.

Bearing in mind that creditors relate to purchases whereas debtors relate to sales, the comments made above at page 124 regarding the weaknesses of an average calculation and the more appropriate "countback" method are equally relevant to the calculation of creditor payment period.

However, there is an additional problem in the measurement of creditor payment period. In addition to normal routine purchases of materials, supplies and services, the figure for creditors may also contain amounts outstanding in respect of irregular payments such as capital expenditure or VAT settlement. Furthermore, the accountant, for convenience, may have included in the figure for creditors some accrued liabilities, e.g. in respect of unpaid wages or overhead items as described on page 26. Clearly these non-routine items must be disclosed separately from routine creditor payment statistics.

Management of Trade Creditors

Supplier credit is a most valuable means both of reducing working capital and providing "free" finance. For this reason some unscrupulous firms deliberately delay payment to small suppliers in particular—sometimes small suppliers have been tipped into bankruptcy by such action. It is right and proper to *negotiate* the longest possible credit terms with suppliers and subsequently to ensure that this credit is taken in full: this is trade credit management; breaking contractual agreements and unjustifiably delaying payment is not.

Unjustifiable taking of credit from suppliers could actually turn out to be far from "free" finance if the supplier retaliates by cutting off supplies or increasing prices to offset the cost of providing this "free" finance to the customer.

The comments made above at page 126 about the correct evaluation of cash discounts are equally valid here. It would be well worth your borrowing money at 18 percent p.a. to pay a supplier who is offering you 2½ percent discount if you pay in 10 days instead of 30 (which we demonstrated on page 126 is equivalent to your earning 46 percent p.a.).

"Package Deals"

We have established that working capital is expensive to carry. We have also looked at the ways in which the individual elements of working capital can best be managed. However, it might be rewarding to look at working capital *as a whole* in addition to looking at its individual elements separately.

What is the relationship between our stock and work in progress, trade debtors and trade creditors and what is the same relationship in the accounts of both our suppliers and our customers? Perhaps there could be benefit to all parties by negotiating total package deals which, in addition to price, would consider, for example, who carries the stock and where; what delivery and batch size arrangements are the most advantageous to all parties; what is the most efficient chain of credit terms. Bearing in mind that one firm's debtor is another firm's creditor and that stock reductions by the supplier might mean stock increases to the customer, there is a distinct possibility that unnecessary duplication of working capital occurs at every step in the supply chain. In such a case, the only one who gains is the bank manager who is financing this unnecessary working capital all the way down the chain.

CHAPTER 14

Principles of Absorption Cost Accounting

CHAPTER 1 outlined the twin fields of accounting. Financial accounting has already been considered in some detail and now the field of management accounting will be explored.

Deficiency of Annual Accounts

Financial accounting is geared to the ultimate preparation of annual accounts which are an indispensable aid to an appreciation of the financial position of a business. However, as an aid to day-to-day management, they present two serious disadvantages:

1. They are historical. If the situation is bad, corrective action should be taken by management long before annual accounts are prepared (in fact management often produces a profit and loss account and balance sheet more frequently than once per year—ideally monthly).

2. They are global. Management is concerned with detailed, or segmental, operating results of each aspect of business activities in addition to the overall position revealed by annual accounts.

Consider the following simplified profit statement of a firm selling three products:

	£
Sales	2,000
Operating expenses	1,600
Operating profit	£400

An operating profit to sales ratio of 20 percent may appear reasonable, but a different picture is obtained if an analysis of the figures is available:

	Total as above £	Product analysis A £	B £	C £
Sales	2,000	800	700	500
Operating expenses	1,600	400	900	300
Operating profit	£400	£400	£(200)	£200

Product B is heavily subsidized by products A and C. This may be unavoidable or even established policy (discussed more fully in the next chapter), but if the information is available, management is at least made aware of the situation and is then able to take whatever action it can.

Clearly there is need for something additional to financial accounts if management is to make the best use of its accounting service. This need is filled by management accounting (or cost accounting), which provides up-to-date accounting information on the detailed operating results of individual jobs, products, processes, departments or any other segment of business activities.

Segmental Profit

For purposes of illustration in this chapter let us assume that management is interested in the operating profit of individual jobs and in particular of job 616, an engineering product.

How may this profit be ascertained? Every item of operating expense incurred by the firm could be considered, those relating to job 616 added together and the difference between the total thus obtained and the selling price of the job would be its operating profit. This requires a tremendous feat of analysis and is impracticable, however desirable it may be. To cut down the work involved, certain short cuts are adopted in practice, although the basic object is still to add together all items of expense relevant to job 616.

Direct Costs

The first step is to separate, evaluate and add together those items which can be traced conveniently and directly to the job. These items are of three types and will be obtained as indicated:

1. *Direct labour*. Productive labour hours directly employed on this job are obtained from time sheets or job cards or other records completed by operatives and priced at the appropriate wage rate.

2. *Direct material*. Quantities of material directly used on this job are obtained from stores requisitions, material specifications or other stores documentation and priced at the appropriate price of the material used.

3. *Direct expenses*. Any other expenditure incurred specifically for this job—for example, special tools or hire of special equipment—is obtained from relevant invoices or receipted accounts.

Only operatives directly working on the conversion of direct material into the finished product can be regarded as direct labour. All other labour is classified as "indirect labour" and will be included in indirect expenses (see below). Similarly, only material which can be directly identified with a particular job is regarded as direct. All other material is classified as "indirect material" and is also included in indirect expenses.

Furthermore, only those items which can be traced easily and conveniently to a job are regarded as direct items. Somewhere in job 616 there may be a touch of grease, taken from a drum issued from stores for general use in an assembly shop: it would be impracticable to attempt to assess the cost of this touch of grease, even though it has been directly used on the job. Such material would, for convenience, be regarded as indirect.

The total of direct items is also referred to as the *prime cost* of a job.

Indirect Expense (Overheads)

After dealing with the direct cost there remains a large volume of expenditure which cannot easily be traced directly to a particular job because it is incurred generally for the benefit of all jobs. Within this group would be included such items as general shop-floor labour, supervision, materials which cannot be related directly to a job, management salaries, heat, light, power, depreciation and general establishment charges. These are termed indirect expenses or *overheads*.

A big problem now is to decide what proportion of overhead shall be included in the cost of job 616—or, to introduce further technical terms, what proportion of overhead shall be *absorbed* by, or *recovered* by, job 616. A simple solution is to add some percentage, based on past experience, to prime cost. An analysis of operating expenses charged in last year's profit and loss account, for example, might reveal the following:

	£
Direct cost	1,233
Overheads	3,699
Total operating expenses	£4,932

Overhead is thus 300 percent of direct cost, which could be used as a basis for overhead absorption as follows:

	Job A	Job B
	£	£
Direct labour	50	50
Direct material	100	100
Direct cost	150	150
Overhead 300%	450	450
Total cost	£600	£600

Job A was carried out by a skilled man, whose wage rate is £20 per hour, working on an expensive machine for 2.5 hours and using 10 kilos of material costing £10 per kilo. Job B is a dissimilar job which was carried out by an apprentice, whose wage rate is £2 per hour, working on a small machine for 25 hours: he spoilt the job once and had to start all over again and, in all, he used 1000 kilos of material costing 10p per kilo.

In the light of all the facts, is it reasonable that both jobs should bear the same amount of overhead? Surely not: the flat percentage method of absorption has avoided the true incidence of overhead by ignoring three vital facts:

1. Overhead is not incurred uniformly throughout the firm: some sections are more expensive to operate than others.

2. Overhead is often incurred in service departments; different jobs or different segments of the production process might make very different calls on these services.

3. A large part of overhead is incurred in relation to the passage of time; the longer a job takes, the greater should be the overhead absorption.

Therefore, a method of absorption must be found which acknowledges these facts.

Analysis of Overhead

Overhead must be absorbed not in one but in several stages in order to accord with fact No. 1 and 2 above and to get away from the global approach. For this reason, overhead is analysed into a small number of groups which correspond to the main sections of activity within the firm. Each group of overhead is then absorbed separately into the cost of the job.

The groups selected will be determined by the organization of the firm and by the nature of business carried on, but a common selection is: *production overhead, administration overhead, selling overhead* and *distribution overhead.* Each item of expense forming part of the overhead must be allocated primarily to one of these groups or, where necessary, analysed between two or more (as in the case of rent: that proportion attributable to the works is production overhead, whereas that attributable to showrooms is selling overhead and so on).

Absorption of Production Overhead

Production overhead is that part of overhead which is incurred in operating the production departments (e.g. general shop floor labour; supervision; rent, rates, heat and light of factory areas; depreciation of productive plant and machinery). It must be absorbed by the jobs which are passing through the production departments whilst the overhead is being incurred; moreover, the basis of absorption selected must take account of the passage of time. All this can be achieved by calculating an hourly rate of production overhead and each job will then absorb its share of production overhead by applying this hourly rate to the number of hours the job spends in production. The hourly rate will be calculated by applying the formula:

$$\frac{\text{estimate of production overhead to be incurred in any period}}{\text{estimate of hours of production in same period}}$$

However, this method of absorption, whilst taking account of the passage of time, ignores the other vital fact: that overhead is not incurred uniformly throughout the firm. It is obviously inequitable to charge the same amount of production overhead to a job engaging a hand operation for 10 hours as to a job engaging a costly precision machine for 10 hours. This problem is overcome in practice by calculating separate production overhead absorption rates (*cost rates* for short) for each section of production activity, each machine if necessary, instead of the one global rate referred to above.

Cost Rates

Calculation of cost rates resolves itself into six distinct stages:

1. *Estimate of production overhead.* A detailed estimate is built up item by item for the period under review.

2. *Allocation to departments.* Production overhead estimated under 1 is allocated, on varying bases, according to the nature of each individual item of expense, over the various departments in the works. Distinction is drawn between *production departments* (where the work is actually produced) and *service departments* (auxiliary departments, such as boiler house and maintenance, which provide a service for the production departments).

3. *Reallocation of service department cost.* The total overhead allocated to each service department under 2 is reallocated to production departments in proportion to the amount of service rendered by the service department to each production department.

4. *Allocation to cost centres.* Because production overhead is not even incurred uniformly throughout the production department, each department is further subdivided into cost centres. A *cost centre* is the smallest production unit to which costs can conveniently be allocated and within which there is homogeneity of production method. Thus a cost centre may consist of one machine, or a group of similar machines, or a collection of hand labour performing similar tasks. The total overhead allocated to each production department under 2 and 3 is now further allocated, on similar bases, to cost centres within each production department.

5. *Estimate of production hours.* An estimate is made of the hours to be spent on production in each cost centre during the period under review. Note that it is the hours to be spent on production which must be estimated, i.e. after anticipating holidays, waiting time, breakdowns and other unproductive time.

6. *Calculation of cost rates.* For each cost centre, the estimated overhead from 4 is divided by the estimated hours from 5 to arrive at an hourly production overhead absorption rate.

It will be apparent from the above (particularly from the vital steps 1 and 5) that a cost rate is an estimate prepared in advance of a defined period of time for use during that period of time.

Production overhead will now be absorbed cost centre by cost centre instead of globally, as first suggested on page 133. For example, if job 616 has spent 4 hours in cost centre 106, 2 hours in cost centre 207 and 5 hours in 210, the amount of production overhead absorbed is: 4 × hourly cost rate for cost centre 106, plus 2 × rate for 207, plus 5 × rate for 210.

The number of hours a job spends in each cost centre will already be available, because this information has been ascertained previously for the purposes of charging direct labour to the job. A single cost rate incorporating both direct labour and production overhead is commonly used in practice to avoid the necessity of performing two multiplications using the same multiplier.

Production Overhead Allocation

Before going on to consider absorption of the other groups of overhead, a digression will be made into the bases of allocation employed at stages 2, 3 and 4 in the calculation of cost rates.

The main object is to ensure that the allocation, as near as possible, reflects the facts. An actual basis must therefore be used wherever possible: for example, depreciation and power of machines can be allocated directly to the appropriate cost centre; wages of a labourer can be allocated directly to the department within which he works; boiler fuel is a cost of operating the boiler house and will be allocated direct to that service department. However, there will remain a large number of items which cannot be allocated directly to a particular department or cost centre; some equitable basis of apportionment must be adopted for these items which will reflect the estimated benefit derived by each department or cost centre. A few examples are tabulated below to indicate the various bases of apportionment which are adopted in practice.

Suggested basis	Suitable for
Proportionate to effective floor space occupied	Rent, rates and upkeep of buildings, lighting* and heating*
Proportionate to number of employees	Canteen, welfare, time keepers, supervision
Proportionate to number of hours worked	Sundry small items
Technical estimate or past experience	Maintenance, internal transport and other services, works management

* If actual metered consumption per department is not available.

Forms which can be used to assist in allocating production overhead and in calculating cost rates are reproduced on pages 137 and 138.

Cost of Production

This is the term applied to that stage in cost ascertainment which reflects the accumulated cost of the product coming off the shop floor, i.e. prime cost plus production overhead.

Absorption of Administration Overhead

Administration overhead includes general office salaries, postage and stationery, rent, rates, heat and light of office area, office cleaning and depreciation and maintenance of office equipment.

A considerable amount of cold water was poured on the flat percentage method of overhead absorption in earlier pages, and yet it is this very method which is most often used for absorption of that part of overhead incurred in general administration. The percentage which is adopted is usually applied to cost of production. Those in favour of this method argue that the administrative machinery is maintained to administer the production processes, and so the higher the cost of production, the higher should be the cost of administration. The ready acceptance of this method dates from the time when administration overhead was of negligible amount compared with the cost of production: any more elaborate method of absorption would have cost too much to administer in relationship to the benefits to be derived.

However, the weight of administration overhead is growing in modern business as sophisticated control techniques are developed, computers are employed and automation in the factory creates fewer jobs for shop-floor workers and more jobs for salaried technicians. The time is overdue when a more equitable basis of absorption must be found for administration overhead. It is in situations such as this where Activity Based Costing (see page 142) has found application.

It may well be difficult to select an equitable basis for absorption for the bulk of administration overhead, but this is no excuse for not seriously considering the problem. Perhaps the answer is to shift the emphasis from absorption to control. Is the particular element of administration overhead really necessary? Is value for money being obtained? These questions will be considered further in Chapter 16 under the heading of budgetary control.

PRODUCTION OVERHEAD

Departmental Allocation Schedule

Period ending ....

Item	Total	Basis of allocation	Production departments				Service departments		
			Light M/c	Heavy M/c	Assembly	Etc.	Boiler house	Maintenance	Etc.
	£		£	£	£	£	£	£	£
Rates	4,000	Floor area	1,000	2,000	480	300	40	80	100
Power	4,320	Metered consumption	1,140	2,090	590	—	450	50	—
Lighting	1,000	Number of points	150	200	400	150	25	50	25
Boiler fuel	4,180	Boiler house	—	—	—	—	4,180	—	—
General labour	8,600	Actual	1,000	1,200	1,600	800	900	2,250	850
National insurance	1,000	Actual	250	250	250	100	25	50	75
General insurance	3,070	Insured values	1,091	1,636	109	50	109	55	20
Depreciation	7,743	Actual plant installed	2,333	3,250	850	180	800	250	80
Supervision	7,950	Actual	1,500	1600	1,600	1,250	700	800	500
Works management	5,000	Time occupied estimate	1,000	1,000	1,000	500	50	1,000	450
Sundries	750	Past experience	250	250	100	75	15	50	10
Total expense	47,613		9,714	13,476	6,979	3,405	7,294	4,635	2,110
Reallocations:									
Boiler house	—	Process steam: actual (metered)		2,000		500	-2,600		100
		Heating: floor area	1,185	2,370	570	355	-4,694	95	119
Maintenance	—	Technical estimate	1,200	2,200	900	400		-4,730	30
Etc.	—	Etc.	800	800	400	359			-2,359
Total allocation	£47,613		£12,899	£20,846	£8,849	£5,019	—	—	—

LIGHT MACHINING DEPARTMENT

Production Overhead Allocation and Cost Rate Calculation   *Period ending* . . . .

Items allocated per departmental allocation schedule	Total	Basis of allocation	Cost centres				
			1 Centre lathes	2 Turret lathes	3 Horiz. miller	4 Grinder universal	Etc. Etc.
	£		£	£	£	£	£
Rates	1,000	Floor area	200	200	150	50	400
Power	1,140	Metered or H.P. hrs.	320	370	60	120	270
Lighting	150	Floor area	30	30	22	8	60
General labour	1,000	Management estimate	300	200	200	100	200
National insurance	250	Hours of production	60	40	36	12	102
General insurance	1,091	Insured values	300	500	150	100	41
Depreciation	2,333	Actual	640	1,075	320	215	83
Supervision	1,500	Number of employees	300	225	150	75	750
Works management	1,000	Number of employees	200	150	100	50	500
Sundries	250	Hours of production	60	40	36	12	102
Heating (boiler house)	1,185	Floor area	238	238	178	60	471
Maintenance	1,200	Technical estimate	330	300	370	100	100
Etc.	800	Etc.	300	200	200	100	—
Total expense	**£12,899**	*a*	£3,278	£3,568	£1,972	£1,002	£3,079
No. of machines in cost centre			3	2	2	1	5
Estimated hours of production		*b*	500	340	300	100	850
Hourly Cost Rate		*a ÷ b*	£6.56	£10.49	£6.57	£10.02	£3.62

Absorption of Selling Overhead

This is also a difficult problem, dealing as it does with such items as advertising, salaries, commission and expenses of sales force, rent, rates, heat, light and upkeep of showrooms. How can this be related to the cost of a particular job or product when there is no direct relationship between the amount of selling effort required and the ultimate sale achieved? Many long and expensive visits may be made which produce nothing and yet a brief telephone inquiry may bring home a large order.

If the efforts of certain parts of the sales force are devoted to selling a particular product group, a primary allocation of selling overhead should be made to that product group. Similarly the cost of a special advertising campaign or sales drive for the benefit of one product would be allocated to that product. However, absorption into the cost of a job still remains a problem which again is often solved by applying a percentage, calculated separately for each product group, to sales value or cost of production.

Attention was drawn above to the problem posed by the growing weight of administration overhead in modern business. Selling overhead is growing even faster as, over the years, there has been an increasing recognition of the importance of the marketing aspects of a business organization.

With the emergence of an increasingly developed and complex economy due to a vast increase in the number of firms competing in the same markets, businessmen have been forced, to a greater or lesser extent, to change their philosophy from "we must sell what we can make" to "we must make what we can sell". The implication is that whoever satisfies best the demands of the market will be most successful. Thus more time, effort and money have been spent on ascertaining the needs of the market and this has resulted in a variety of specialist marketing functions such as market research, motivation research, advertising (press, poster, TV, cinema, magazines, etc.) and sales promotion. No longer, in the present state of intense competition, will "the world beat a path to the door of the man who makes a better mousetrap" (to paraphrase Emerson). Manufacturers must now distinguish their product from a host of others in the eyes of the consuming public and, increasingly as more nations become industrialized, in the eyes of industrial goods users also.

A most significant recent trend indicates that it is becoming increasingly less profitable to indulge in a constant battle to maintain or improve one's market position. Thus there is emerging a philosophy of regular introduction of new products in the hope that during the first year or two of the sales life of the product the innovating firm will have a virtual monopoly—since it takes that length of time for competitors successfully to launch a competing product. In this way the innovating firm will reap the "monopoly profit". When strong competition arises, the time has come to introduce another product and so on—always striving to keep ahead of the market. Perhaps the following diagram more adequately describes this product life cycle:

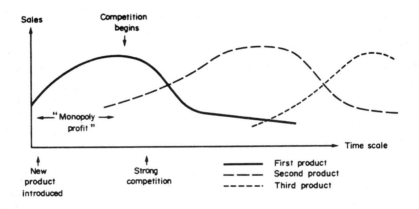

Therefore in addition to increasing marketing costs there is an increasing amount spent on research and development to ensure that the firm stays one jump ahead by always having a "new" product in the pipeline ready for the market. Whether research and development cost are properly regarded as part of selling overhead or of production overhead or treated separately is a matter of opinion—the problem of absorption remains.

The general field of selling overhead therefore embraces expenditures which are increasing at a relatively stupendous rate in many industries. By their very weight they thus require a treatment different from the time-honoured percentage absorption approach. Certainly more direct bases of absorption must be used but, as with administration overhead, perhaps the answer is partly to shift the emphasis from absorption to control. Again the questions—is the expenditure really necessary?, is value for money being obtained? Certain control techniques are considered in Chapter 16.

Absorption of Distribution Overhead

Yet another costly area of the burden of overhead is that of distribution, which includes packing, freight, transit insurance and upkeep of despatch warehouse and transport department. Distribution will normally be peculiar to a particular job or product and it should therefore be possible to calculate a reasonably accurate charge per item as a basis of absorption of this group of overhead.

Activity Based Costing

Although the name is relatively new, Activity Based Costing (ABC) is not really "new". It is just a refined basis of absorption costing.

Comments have been made earlier in this chapter about the growth in overheads in proportion to direct cost and the associated difficulty in finding an equitable means of absorbing such overheads into product costs. If total prime, or direct, cost is £500 and total overheads are £50, then a cavalier approach to overhead absorption is more acceptable than if total prime, or direct, cost is £500 and total overheads are £2,000. In the latter case it is necessary to try harder to find an equitable basis for departmental overhead absorption. This is where ABC has found application.

ABC attempts to *relate* the overhead cost of a service department to a production unit or product rather than *absorb* it. In essence ABC seeks first to identify what activities a service department performs and hence what drives the overhead cost of that department (for example the stores department cost may be driven by the quantity of goods received and stores issued). By attaching an overhead cost to such drivers it is possible to follow these through to the production units or products which make use of these cost drivers and so a more equitable basis of relating overheads to products is found.

ABC will never solve the whole difficulty of overhead absorption; there will always be some hard core (e.g. the cost of the Chairman's office) which defies logical relation to an individual production unit or product. But at least ABC will encourage the management accountant to try harder and so reduce the area of cavalier overhead absorption methods.

Total Absorbed Cost

This term refers to the grand total of all direct and absorbed costs and, when compared to selling price, the profit or loss on the job is revealed.

A cost sheet is used in practice to accumulate all these items of cost. A specimen cost sheet is not reproduced because the layout depends so much on the nature of the business carried on, but the chart on page 143 summarizes the routine for ascertaining total cost and profit of any particular job. The chart also shows the relationship between the various technical terms introduced in this chapter.

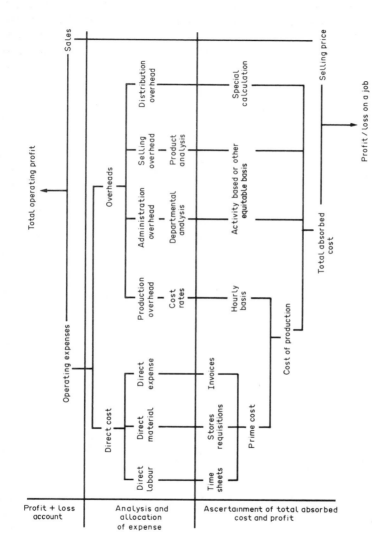

Cost accounting routine for ascertaining profit on a job

CHAPTER 15

Principles of Marginal Costing

A MANAGING director may turn to his works manager and ask, "What are the dimensions of job 616?" The works manager's reply will be accurate to within certain clearly defined tolerances of measurement. If the managing director then asks his cost accountant, "What is the cost of job 616?", there is great danger that the managing director will assume that the reply given possesses the same degree of accuracy as the works manager's reply—which of course it does not.

Accurate Cost?

How reliable is a figure of cost? Before answering, the question must be put more specifically: which cost is required—prime cost, cost of production, total absorbed cost, or what? Prime cost should be reasonably reliable within the limitation of using money as a means of evaluation, whereas cost of production and total absorbed cost are not so reliable.

Reflect for a moment on the chart on page 143 and consider how many estimates, opinions, allocations, apportionments and, of necessity, inspired guesses have gone into the ascertainment of cost of production and total absorbed cost. The cumulative effect of all these cannot possibly produce an "accurate cost" and it is vital to bear this in mind always when dealing with this type of information. Any segmental cost is useful as a guide and as a means of comparison and it must always be treated with the utmost respect.

Accurate Profit?

Blind reliance upon costing figures has sometimes been the cause of business failure. Once one has assumed that costing figures are "accurate", it is but a short step to assume that if the costing figures reveal a reasonable profit on each job, the year-end profit will similarly be reasonable: indeed, the total of all the profits made on individual jobs should equal the operating profit eventually shown in the profit and loss account. This assumption is also unfounded.

There are two main reasons why the total of all the profits made on individual jobs (costing profit) might not agree with the operating profit revealed by the profit and loss account (financial profit):

1. For domestic or political reasons, certain items of expense may be excluded from the costing figures (e.g. research expenditure); on the other hand notional items of expense may be included in the costing figures (e.g. internal rental or interest charges) which do not appear in the financial figures. As this is a policy decision, management is fully aware that the ultimate financial profit will be costing profit plus or minus these items and this will be taken into account when determining the profit margin for individual jobs.

2. Over-and under-absorption of overhead. This is the aspect of the problem which can prove fatal to a business if management is not kept informed of its extent.

Under-absorption of Overhead

Certain estimates were made in compiling overhead absorption rates. If the estimates prove correct, the actual overhead incurred will be fully absorbed in the cost of completed jobs; if the estimates prove incorrect, there will be either an over- or an under-absorption of overhead. Consider the following example:

Estimate of overhead	£1500
Estimate of hours of production	1000 hours
Overhead absorption rate	£1.50 per hour
Actual overhead	£1000
Actual hours of production	500 hours

In this example, overhead absorbed will be 500 hours @ £1.50 or £750 whilst the actual overhead is £1000: an under-absorption of £250. Costing profit will thus be overstated by £250. This example is over simplified in that one overhead absorption rate has been used. When all the stages of overhead absorption noted in the chart on page 143 are in use, each stage requires estimates to be made and each estimate may be wrong. Thus the situation is infinitely complex in practice but is vitally important in view of the danger of believing that profits are being earned when in fact the business is making a loss—a fool's paradise indeed.

There is, of course, the other side to the coin: it is possible to over-absorb. Management is no less concerned with this state of affairs, which may have an important bearing on pricing policy.

Reconciliation of Profit

A special exercise should be carried out frequently, say once a month, reconciling the financial profit with the costing profit and bringing out the reasons for any disparity. It must not be assumed that costing is a waste of time because this reconciliation is necessary. Indeed this exercise adds to the value of the costing service by indicating its tolerances of accuracy and, by making minor adjustments, the value of the service as a management aid is greatly enhanced.

Fixed and Variable Expenses

One of the causes of under-absorption is that when hours of production are reduced, overhead does not necessarily reduce in the same proportion. This is because some expenses tend to be fixed and some tend to be variable.

Fixed expenses are those which *tend* to remain fixed, irrespective of variations in volume of output—e.g. rent, rates, salaries, depreciation. Sometimes referred to as *period costs* or *policy costs*.

Variable expenses are those which *tend* to vary directly with variations in volume of output—e.g. power, consumable stores, all direct material. Sometimes referred to as *direct costs* or *marginal costs*.

Fixed expenses are thus related to a period of time irrespective of volume of output whilst variable expenses are related to volume of output irrespective of time. Observe the use of the word "tends" in the above definitions. One cannot dogmatize and state categorically that this item is always fixed and that is always variable. Indeed, in the short run everything may well be fixed (can labour and materials be disposed of at a moment's notice?) but in the long run everything is variable (as when all expense is terminated by closing down the business). An item may be fixed under certain circumstances but variable under others. For example, works supervision is normally fixed irrespective of variations in volume of output.

However, if a variation in output entails the acquisition of further manufacturing capacity or the introduction of shift working, an increase in supervision will be necessary. Under these circumstances works supervision ceases to be fixed at the base level. Some accountants widen the classification by also grouping expense under terms such as *semi-variable*, *semi-fixed* or *stepped*, indicating that whilst there is variation, it is not related directly to variation in volume of output.

This book will not dwell on fine academic points: all that is required of the reader for an appreciation of what follows is a general understanding of the fundamental distinction between fixed and variable expenses.

Significance of Volume

Absorption rates for overhead are compiled for an estimated volume of output. It is therefore apparent that if there is a significant variation from that estimate the rates will become unrealistic. Furthermore, when there is a substantial amount of fixed expense, any significant variation in volume of output will have a significant effect upon total unit cost: the higher the volume, the lower the fixed expense per unit of output ... and vice versa.

For example, a firm with fixed expenses of £100 and variable expenses of £1 per unit will be affected by variations in volume as follows:

Output in units	10	20	100
	£	£	£
Fixed expenses	100	100	100
Variable expenses	10	20	100
Total expenses	£110	£120	£200
Cost per unit	£11	£6	£2

This simple matter plays an important part in guiding management decisions:

Picture the scene: the marketing manager is about to take an important pricing decision and therefore asks the cost accountant "What is the cost of this product?"; "Anything from £11 to £2" comes his reply, quickly adding "Provided that there has been no error in any of the many estimates and opinions underlying the several bases of allocation and absorption of overhead which have been used."

The Argument for Marginal Costing

What price absorption costing as a basis for guiding management decisions of the type just exemplified? Consider the following arguments:

1. Management decisions, as far as possible, should be guided by fact rather than by opinion.

2. An absorbed cost of necessity must be a mixture of fact (mainly in the direct cost area) and of opinion (mainly in the allocation and absorption of overhead).

3. The proportion of overhead, and therefore of opinion, in total absorbed costs tends to grow over time and as a business develops, thereby aggravating the problem.

4. Many cost accountants are burning midnight oil in the compilation of absorption cost rates and total absorbed costs which subsequently might be of little practical assistance to management decision taking.

These rather powerful arguments are used by the advocates of marginal (or direct) costing, the essential elements of which can be summarized as follows:

1. it tries to stick to facts and avoid the need to express opinions;

2. it tries to avoid the need to allocate or absorb overhead;

3. it sees operating profit not so much as sales minus operating expenses but as a two-stage process:

    (a) sales minus direct expenses equals *contribution*, sometimes referred to as *gross margin*, or *margin*

    (b) contribution minus overheads equals operating profit;

4. segmental analysis is taken only as far as contribution, not all the way down to operating profit.

The tables on page 149 summarize the difference in approach between absorption and marginal costing. The most significant attribute of marginal costing is that it sees operating profit as the difference between contribution and overheads, i.e. there are only two routes to the creation of operating profit:

either increase contribution,
or reduce overheads

There are several ways of doing each of these, of course, but broadly speaking increasing contribution or reducing overheads are the only things

Absorption costing

	Total	Segmental analysis			
	£	£	£	£	£

Sales

Deduct:
  Prime cost items
  Production overhead

Gross profit

Deduct non-production expenses:
  Administration
  Selling
  Distribution

Operating profit

Note that all costs are spread to the segmental analysis: prime cost items on a Factual basis, overheads on some equitable (opinion) basis.

Marginal costing

	Total	Segmental analysis			
	£	£	£	£	£

Sales

Deduct:
  Direct costs (whether production or elsewhere)

Contribution

Deduct overheads
  (Indirect costs)
  – Production
  – Administration
  – Selling
  – Distribution

Operating profit

Note that only direct costs are spread to the segmental analysis. Overheads are not spread but are reported in total only.

that can be done to create operating profit. (No amount of reallocation of overhead will create real operating profit.) At this stage the reader is invited to return to page 115: the logic of structuring the left-hand side of the financial fault-finding chart below ratio no. 2 is perhaps now apparent; no explanation was given at the time.

Use of Marginal Costing

Marginal costing is generally seen as being most appropriate in the guidance of management decisions. If we accept that the only two routes to the creation of operating profit are an increase in contribution or a reduction in overheads, it follows that marginal costing is more appropriate in the guidance of management decisions because it highlights the impact of the decision upon these two elements. We will return to this matter in the next chapter but in the meantime a simple example will suffice. "The cost" (i.e. total absorbed cost) of an item is £10 and the best price obtainable in the market-place is £8. Should the opportunity to sell be accepted or rejected? Absorption costing might suggest rejection in the light of the £2 "loss". But suppose that this £10 total absorbed cost was made up of direct cost £7 and absorption of fixed overhead £3. In this case marginal costing might suggest acceptance because sale at £8 would at least create a contribution of £1 (£8-£7 direct cost) towards the totality of fixed overheads, i.e. contribution and therefore operating profit will be higher by £1 as a result of a sale at £8 than with no sale at all—unless of course overheads could be reduced by £1 if the sale were not made.

Dangers of Marginal Costing

Having put forward the arguments for marginal costing and against absorption costing it is perhaps fair to draw attention to the very real dangers in the *uncontrolled* use of marginal costing to guide management decisions.

1. If the simple example above is taken to its illogical conclusion, everything will be sold at deep cut prices which, although producing a small contribution on each item sold, might not add up to the total overheads thereby encouraging a loss to develop.

2. Acceptance of marginal business (i.e. that which is priced very low but still produces a contribution) might not be a good thing even though it does genuinely add to contribution because it may encourage more and more

similarly priced business, eventually pushing out the good until the situation at 1 is created. The object of the exercise must be to increase long-run operating profit—no one should become a busy fool.

3. Business may in fact be obtained at a very good rate of contribution but not in sufficient volume to produce a total contribution sufficiently in excess of overheads to provide an acceptable level of operating profit.

4. Contribution both in detail and in total may appear desirable in the light of a current target but in the meantime overheads may have escalated to a level higher than total contribution—again a negative operating profit.

5. Marginal costing rests largely upon the concept of fixed and variable expense definition, but the point was made earlier in this chapter that no item of expense is either wholly fixed or wholly variable for all time and in all circumstances: therefore outdated marginal cost information might be even less valuable than absorption cost information.

6. There are occasions (e.g. in costs plus pricing decisions) when total absorbed cost data is vital to management: on such occasions, marginal costing is of little value.

Those who use marginal costing therefore must use it with care. Particularly if it is used as part of an ongoing costing system (as opposed to being used solely to guide *ad hoc* short-term management decisions) it must be supported by efficient budgetary control techniques designed to give early warning of the dangers listed above.

Benefits of Costing

In this chapter the limitations of cost accounting have been demonstrated. An attempt has also been made to show how these limitations, if recognized and revealed, can be used to make cost accounting of greater value as a tool of management control. However, in view of the stress which has been placed on these limitations it is appropriate to end this chapter with a list of the benefits one would expect to accrue from the costing service:

1. Profitable and unprofitable segments of a business are disclosed. Steps can be taken to curtail unprofitable activities, or put them on to a profitable basis.

2. Details of all items contributing to total cost of each segment are produced. This will indicate to management any sources of economy which may be effected due to inefficient use of labour, materials, machinery or equipment.

3. An efficient system of stores accounting is essential to the ascertainment of material costs. A more effective control over stocks is thus provided: obsolete and slow-moving stocks are brought to light and the amount of capital tied up in stocks and work in progress is kept to a minimum.

4. Information is made available which will assist the reliable preparation of estimates and tenders.

5. Data are made available from which useful comparisons may be drawn—for example, upon the relative efficiencies of different departments and the relative merits of making or buying certain components.

6. Vital assistance is rendered in the preparation of annual accounts and it is possible to prepare accounts at much more frequent intervals.

Intelligent utilization of the information obtained from the costing service is essential if the maximum benefit is to be obtained. A costing system, similarly to a financial accounting system, must be "tailor-made" to suit the requirements of each firm—it need not be an expensive system, but any expense of operating the system should be adequately justified by the benefits derived.

Management accounting is an investment—the dividends paid thereon can be great indeed.

CHAPTER 16

Accounting as an Aid to Management Planning and Control

IN THE previous chapter the limitations of cost accounting were demonstrated. An attempt was also made to show how these limitations, if recognized and revealed, can be harnessed to make management accounting of greater value as a tool of management control. This chapter will explore some management control techniques which have been developed from cost accounting. A further object of this chapter is to help the reader to appreciate that business accounting is not purely historical but has a vital role to play in current control and future planning of operations.

Need for Planning and Control

Any business activity must be planned. However, although all managements plan, there are considerable differences in the way they plan and the extent of their plans. Managers of the smallest business, having done their planning in the head, may keep all plan details in the head; others may perform rough calculations on the backs of used envelopes.

As a business grows in size and complexity, responsibility must be delegated and personal lines of control are severed. Those at the top no longer have everything at their fingertips, and similarly one particular manager may not be aware of the detailed actions of fellow managers. Under these circumstances there is a compelling need to formalize planning procedures and control techniques. Such formalization necessitates reducing policies, plans and procedures to paper so that all involved in the various activities have the same references and guide lines from which to work.

Planning and control embraces the following aspects:

1. *Long-term planning* on a strategic basis which looks at the firm, its markets and its environment over a number of years ahead in order to

153

develop an overall corporate strategy for the firm's long-term growth and development.

2. *Project planning* (including capital expenditure budgeting) which forecasts how future cash flows will be affected over the life of a specific project or development. Each project under consideration will, of course, be linked to the long-term plan.

3. *Short-term planning* or budgeting on a tactical basis which takes the first time period of the long-term plan together with all ongoing projects and develops a financial blueprint for achievement of this part of the long-term plan or suggests a basis for its amendment.

4. *Monitoring actual results* on a frequent and regular basis, comparing them to budgets which have been produced and highlighting *variances*, or deviations from plan.

5. *Ongoing control* of day-to-day detailed activities of the business in order to ensure that actual results are in line with the short term plan; or through the development of *Rolling Forecasts* to give the earliest possible warning that either the short, or long-term plan cannot be achieved and perhaps should be revised or updated.

Note how each of these five aspects are interrelated and interdependent.

The subjects of long-term strategic planning and capital expenditure budgeting lie beyond the scope of this book, therefore we look now mainly at the subjects of short-term planning, or budgeting, and control. However we will turn briefly to capital investment appraisal in the next chapter.

Budgeting

A budget is a written plan expressed in quantitative terms. This chapter is primarily concerned with budgets expressed in money terms (a convenient common denominator) although non-monetary quantitative measures are used where appropriate—e.g. number of employees, units of time, units of output. The budget is thus a blueprint for future operations within a selected period of time: month, year or longer. A long-term plan will normally be prepared in general terms to give the overall direction for a number of years ahead. The long term is then broken down into shorter budget periods for more detailed budgeting. Detailed budgets will in fact be prepared for each area of business activity prior to being combined into a master budget to reveal the co-ordinated business plan for the budget period.

Co-ordination of Budgets

No individual aspect of the activities of a business exists in isolation: all affect each other to a greater or lesser extent. This presents an initial problem when budgeting because each budget will interact on every other budget, thus posing the problem "Where shall a start be made?" The answer lies in isolating the *limiting factor* and starting at that point: every other budget should then follow in a logical sequence. The limiting factor may be defined as that factor in the activities of a business which at a particular point in time or over a period will limit the ability of the firm to earn contribution. This factor, which may change from time to time, may be the availability of labour, materials, space or capital depending on current conditions and restrictions. However, under normal competitive business conditions operating in a free and unrestricted economy, the limiting factor will usually be the sales volume which a business can achieve. In the sequence of budgets discussed in the following section, sales volume is assumed to represent the limiting factor and accordingly is the first to be considered.

Sequence of Short-term Budgets

In order to obtain a detailed view of a business it will normally be necessary to prepare the following budgets, each of which must be an honest attempt to forecast and evaluate future activities during the forthcoming budget period. Past results may be used as a guide, but these must be amended in the light of anticipated conditions in the budget period. Within the scope of this book the following budgets can be discussed in the briefest detail only.

Sales budget. This should be prepared in detail in terms of both quantity and value for each product after a careful consideration of market conditions and prospects. As this is assumed to be the limiting factor, sales must be forecast as carefully as possible or all other budgets lose their value. The budget must also indicate the credit terms which it is planned to offer to customers. Since it is not possible, of course, for forecasting to be absolutely accurate, flexible budgets can be constructed to take account of possible fluctuations in sales volume. Flexible budgets are discussed further on page 158/159.

Production budget. The production budget forecasts what is to be produced if the sales budget is to be met but it will take into account management's policy on the holding of finished stocks and work in progress. Thus a production budget of 80 units, prepared in the light of a policy reduction of 20 units finished stock, would meet a sales budget of 100 units. A further matter to be considered when drawing up the production budget is that the sales budget may present a seasonal fluctuation in demand which may not be desirable for production purposes if an even flow of production is considered more economical. In this event the production budget would be drawn up assuming a stable rate of production, creating a budgeted buffer stock to meet the fluctuations in demand presented by the seasonal nature of the sales budget.

Labour requirements budget. This budget forecasts the detailed labour requirements to meet the production budget. Potential recruitments or redundancies will be indicated, as will the need for shift or overtime working. A secondary limiting factor here may cause an amendment to be made to the production budget to take account of necessary subcontracting.

Materials requirements budget. Similarly to the labour requirements budget, this budget forecasts the materials required to meet the production budget.

Purchasing budget. In the same way in which the production budget recognized stock policy in planning to meet the sales budget, so the purchasing budget plans to meet the materials requirements budget. Bulk purchase and other buying policies will also be reflected in this budget. The budget must also indicate the credit terms which it is planned to negotiate with suppliers.

Plant requirements budget. This budget will indicate the availability of plant, machinery and equipment in the light of the production budget. New plant, retirements and major overhauls will all be taken into account. New plant and other fixed assets should be planned on a long-term basis in the *capital expenditure budget.*

Departmental overhead budgets. Every item of overhead is caused by and is controllable by someone within the organization. The area under an individual's control is defined as a *budget centre* and a forecast is made of the cost of operating each budget centre (or department) at the level of activity indicated by the sales budget or production budget. Departmental overhead budgets will embrace the whole spectrum of overhead: production, administration, selling and distribution.

The Master Budget

The detailed budgets enumerated above now contain all the information necessary to compile the master budget, which comprises:

1. Forecast profit and loss account or value added statement for the budget period.
2. Forecast balance sheet as at the end of the budget period.
3. Forecast of cash requirements in detail throughout the budget period.

The master budget is thus the "grand plan" or co-ordinated blueprint of operations for the forthcoming budget period. This is a most critical stage in budgeting because, if the master budget reveals a forecast of an unsatisfactory state of affairs, it may be necessary to start all over again on a different premise in an attempt to improve the situation. The reader may smile at this stage, thinking that budgeting is at best just playing with figures. However, to think this is to fail to realize the vital need for planning in modern business. After all, if one is about to undertake a strange journey does one not study maps to select the most advantageous of several possible routes? Budgets are the maps appropriate to the journey into time that the business is about to undertake.

Having selected the most advantageous route, the next stage is to check and report upon any deviation from that route, to attempt to get back on route or, if the circumstances change, to select a new route (i.e. change the plan).

Budgetary Control

This is the area in which financial planning and control of operations are brought together. Budgetary control takes the detailed short-term budgets and compares them with actual results at frequent intervals (e.g. monthly) throughout the budget period. Similarly the master budget is frequently compared with the actual profit and loss account, balance sheet and cash flow position. The value of budgetary control lies in that it does not stop at mere comparison but looks into the causes of differences between budget and actual performance. Thus managerial attention is directed towards divergencies from plan, and action can be taken to correct the situation whilst there is yet time. This important aspect of budgetary control gives rise to the terms *responsibility accounting* and *management by exception* and indicates the main advantages claimed for budgetary control:

1. Responsibility for each item of expense is identified and control exercised over actual results.
2. Managerial attention is directed towards exceptions where action can be taken quickly to rectify the situation.
3. The process acts as a discipline, stimulating departmental efficiency and more effective utilization of resources.

Unfortunately in practice these advantages are sometimes not realized due to the way in which a system of budgetary control may be administered. All systems are administered by people and thereby suffer from any weaknesses in the administration. Budgets may be set without serious consideration or may be employed as whipping blocks or objects of recriminatory post-mortems to an unjustifiable degree. Worse still, some managers may abdicate their responsibility to manage, throwing all responsibility on "the system". This is a psychological problem and these dangers can only be avoided by education of all concerned (both "controller" and "controlled") into that frame of mind which will help them to employ the system intelligently and judiciously.

Effective Control

An effective system of budgetary control should prompt management action by identifying the cause of each variation from budget and directing attention to either reducing or eliminating or getting better value for expense incurred. A vital principle which must be followed is that no one should be held responsible for something which is not primarily under their control. Towards this end the following should be noted:

1. A budget must never be "imposed from above". It should be prepared in conjunction with the person on whom the control is to be exercised. This person should also agree the budget before it is finally accepted as the basis for control of future operations.

2. Everything is controllable by someone. The budget centre structure must ensure that no item is included in any budget unless it is primarily within the control of the person responsible for that budget centre.

3. Control must recognize changed conditions. A budget is normally prepared in the light of a given volume of sales or production. Should actual volume differ from budgeted volume it is unrealistic to draw comparisons between actual results and the original budget. *Flexible budgetary control*

recognizes this by preparing a range of budgets appropriate to a range of volume. In comparing with actual results, it will select that level of budget appropriate to the level of volume actually achieved. In this way divergencies are genuinely controllable and not merely attributable to an error made by someone who originally estimated volume requirements. If there is a radical change in conditions, quite apart from fluctuations in volume, it may be necessary to *revise* a budget completely. This is often done in practice by, say, a quarterly update of an annual budget or by the preparation of rolling annual forecasts at more frequent intervals than once a year.

4. No one can control the past, only the future. Towards this end control information should be forward looking; for example, there is more merit in presenting information which compares the original budget for the year with the now anticipated outcome for the year than there is with comparing the expired portion of the budget to date with the historical outcome to date. Rolling forecasts are clearly essential if this comparison is to be possible.

Project Planning

As part of, or in addition to, the long-term plan, a manager in business is frequently called upon to decide between competing courses of action. The type of decision inferred by the title "project planning" is the "one-off" policy decision outside the normal daily routine. Examples of such decision might be:

1. Whether to cease to make and instead to buy out a major component.

2. Whether to discontinue a particular area of activity, be it a product, a department or a complete manufacturing activity.

3. Justification for capital expenditure, perhaps also involving a selection between competing capital projects or a decision between the alternatives of buying new capital equipment outright or of financing it through a leasing option (we will look briefly at the mechanics of capital investment appraisal in the next chapter).

The decision the manager makes in these circumstances will affect the profitability of the business perhaps for a long time to come. Therefore, in making such decisions managers must have financial information which will assist them to forecast and evaluate the results of their decisions. However, if it is to be effective, the financial information must be *relevant* to the decision which is to be made.

At this stage the reader's attention is directed again to earlier sections of the text:

"Figures tell one story at once"—page 8.

"Fixed and variable expenses" and "significance of volume"—pages 146–147.

It should now be apparent that financial information must be specially tailored for each special project. Each such project faced in business will normally be concerned with a new set of circumstances. It will be a most unusual coincidence if financial information produced for some other purpose or to assist an earlier piece of project planning will be entirely relevant to the circumstances of the decision now being faced. Hence the excitingly vital element of this aspect of business accounting: sometimes referred to as *incremental analysis*.

Unfortunately the scope of this book does not permit a more thorough investigation into this field nor a detailed description of all the techniques which have been developed to provide financial information in an acceptable form. The object of such techniques is to provide *relevant*, or *incremental*, figures to assess the effect that any decision is likely to have on the financial viability of the business. These figures will reveal what income will be earned in cash, what expenditure will be incurred in cash and what capital outlay will be required as a result of this decision but of no other. Armed with this information the manager can measure the effect that his decision will have on future profitability (as measured by RONA or ROSF) and on future cash flow.

Break-even Analysis

This technique is an offshoot of marginal costing and finds particularly useful application within flexible budgeting and within project planning. Recall from the previous chapter that:

selling price—direct cost = contribution

and   contribution—overheads = operating profit

it therefore follows that:

1. when contribution = overheads, operating profit will be nil (this is called the *Break-even Point*);

2. operating profit + overheads = contribution (a useful rephrasing of the relationship, particularly when used in planning and expressed as: target operating profit + budgeted overheads = the necessary target contribution which must be achieved by the plan);

3. contribution—operating profit = overheads (another useful rephrasing of the relationship when used in planning and expressed as: maximum contribution achievable under the sales budget—target operating profit = maximum overheads that the budgeted level of sales can support).

Let us consider a grossly over-simplified example of break-even analysis: Suppose we were to open a shop to sell that well-known product Plod ... which we can buy at £8 each and sell at £10 each; suppose also that our policy in selecting our shop predetermines our overheads (e.g. rent, heat, light, assistant's wages) at £10,000 p.a.; suppose, also that we desire at least 15 percent p.a. return to satisfy the £40,000 invested in net operating assets for our venture into Plod:

(a) How many Plods must be sold to cover our overheads (i.e. to break even)?
(b) How many Plods must be sold to earn the 15 percent RONA?
(c) If sales potential at a selling price of £10 each is 7000 Plods, what is the maximum permissible spend on overheads?
(d) Is it worth undertaking an advertising campaign at a cost of £500?
(e) Is it worth lowering the selling price by £0.50?

Break-even analysis will help us to reach the answers to these five questions as follows:

(a) This question is asking for the break-even point, i.e. at what volume of Plod does contribution = overheads? Contribution is £2 per Plod (£10 selling price—£8 direct cost) whilst overheads are £10,000. Break-even point is therefore at 5000 units which can be proved as follows:

	£
Sales, 5000 @ £10	50,000
Deduct: direct costs, 5000 @ £8	40,000
overheads	10,000
Operating profit	nil

(b) This question is asking for the application of formula 2 above, i.e. target contribution must equal the target operating profit of £6000 (15 percent RONA on £40,000) plus budgeted overheads of £10,000 which is £16,000 or 8000 Plod and can be proved as follows:

	£
Sales, 8000 @ £10	80,000
Deduct: direct costs, 8000 @ £8	64,000
overheads	10,000
Operating profit	£6,000
Net operating assets	£40,000
RONA (operating profit % net operating assets)	15%

(c) This question is asking for the application of formula 3 above, i.e. maximum achievable contribution is 7000 Plods @ £2 or £14,000—target operating profit of £6,000 = maximum overhead spend of £8,000 and can be proved as follows:

	£
Sales, 7000 @ £10	70,000
Deduct: direct costs, 7000 @ £8	56,000
overheads	8,000
Operating profit	£6,000
Net operating assets	£40,000
RONA	15%

(d) It is worth undertaking the advertising campaign only if it produces additional sales of at least 250 units because these will generate an additional contribution, at £2 each, on £500 which will just pay for the additional overhead of £500 and so maintain the operating profit intact.

(e) The new selling price would reduce contribution to £1.50 per unit; thus it is worth lowering the selling price only if sales volume increases by a sufficient amount to maintain the total contribution intact—returning to questions (a) and (b):

(a) the break-even point now moves up to £10,000 ÷ £1·50 or 6667 units,
(b) the target sales volume now moves up to (£6,000 + £10,000) ÷ £1·50 or 10,667 units.

The Break-even Chart

The underlying relationships of break-even analysis can be expressed graphically in the celebrated break-even chart. Only the most simple versions of this chart will be described here in detail but brief reference will be given later to some of the more practical aspects. The simple break-even chart blindly assumes that expenses are either directly variable or completely fixed and that selling price is constant within a wide range of volume. Let us apply the technique to the well-known product Plod:

1. Direct costs vary at the rate of £8 per unit and can be expressed graphically as follows:

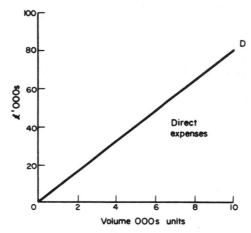

2. Overheads are fixed at £10,000 and can be expressed graphically as follows:

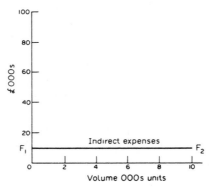

3. Sales at the £10 selling price can be expressed graphically as follows:

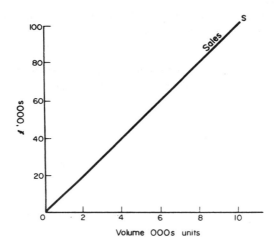

Putting these three graphs together so as to show also the total expenses (i.e. direct costs and overheads added together) we now get the following break-even chart:

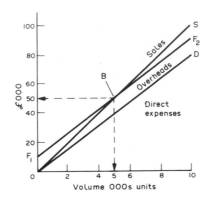

Note that:

(a) angle SOD is contribution,

(b) point B is the break-even point (5000 units as calculated on page 161).

  (c) area F_1BO indicates losses, where contribution fails to cover overheads,

  (d) area SBF_2 indicates operating profit and this amounts to £6000 at 8000 units as calculated on page 162.

A much more simple, two-line break-even chart can be drawn as follows, where line OC is contribution (@ £2 per unit of Plod):

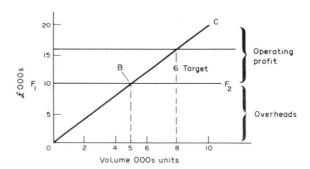

Note that break-even point is again 5000 units, area F_1BO again indicates loss and that operating profit is again £6000 at 8000 units.

Having only two lines, it is possible to test the impact of proposed management decisions much more clearly. For example the impact of the proposed price change in Plod question (e) can be demonstrated as follows, where line OC_1 is the original contribution @ £2 per unit and line OC_2 is the proposed contribution @ £1.50 per unit:

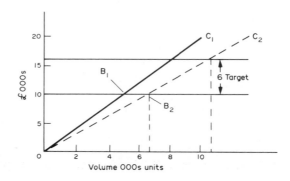

Note that the break-even point now moves out from B_1 6000 units to B_2 6667 units and the target sales volume to 10,667 units as calculated on page 162.

Break-even charting is never as simple as this in practice because direct costs are never directly variable, nor overheads permanently fixed, nor selling prices constant over a wide range of volume. However, the principle of break-even analysis is nevertheless helpful when attempting to find that sensitive, or "go/no go" point upon which an alternative choice management decision might turn.

Margin of Safety

No business wishes to operate at break even: this represents the critical lower level of volume below which it becomes unprofitable to operate. So a useful development of break-even analysis is to compute the *margin of safety* which reveals how far below the current position volume can fall before break-even is reached.

Returning to our well-known product Plod question (a) where we calculated break-even point at 5000 units; if we are currently selling 8000 units, we have a margin of safety of 8000—5000 = 3000 units which is 37.5 percent of the current 8000 units—a handsome margin of safety indeed. On the other hand if we are currently selling 6000 units, our margin of safety is only 1000 units or 16.7 percent of the 6000 currently being sold: if volume falls by more than 16.7 percent we will be operating at a loss.

Alternatively, margin of safety can be indicated by stating the break-even point as a percent of the current sales or percent of capacity: i.e. how many units must be sold before we *start* making a profit. Applying this to the numbers above, the break-even point is 62.5 percent of current sales at 8000 units and 83.3 percent of current sales at 6000 units. This approach is frequently used in similar businesses to airlines: how many "bums on seats", or what percent of capacity must be filled, before a flight becomes profitable?

Some Other Techniques

For the sake of completeness an outline is given below of four financial control techniques employed in business. They are referred to only briefly to whet the reader's appetite for fuller reading in other volumes.

Standard costing goes further than budgetary control and compares predetermined product costs with actual results, operation by operation.

As in budgetary control, managerial action is directed towards any operating deficiencies revealed by the *variances* (differences between predetermined "standard" and actual results) which are thrown up by the system.

Incremental analysis applies the principles of marginal costing and break-even analysis to individual management decisions in such a way as to isolate the true impact of such a decision upon profit, profitability or cash flow. A few examples of decisions which might employ this technique are:

1. In the field of marketing:
   (a) price determination including special pricing, price/volume trade-offs and market segmentation;
   (b) evaluation of special promotions;
   (c) direction of effort to specific products.
2. In the field of purchasing:
   (a) make or buy decisions;
   (b) quantity purchase at advantageous prices versus stock-holding cost;
   (c) special packaging or delivery arrangements.
3. In the field of production:
   (a) allocation of orders to different factories;
   (b) selection of method of manufacture;
   (c) utilization of surplus capacity.

As mentioned earlier in this chapter, the technique finds wide application in project planning.

Opportunity costing is also directed towards assisting management decisions or project planning. It is concerned with comparative rather than actual costs and considers, as part of the cost of any action, the return or value foregone by deciding upon this course of action rather than upon that. For example, the cost of producing X is deemed to be the profit that could have been earned if Y had been produced instead, or if capital had been invested with Z instead, or if some other rewarding opportunity had been seized instead.

Zero base budgeting finds application particularly when budgeting for non-production and service departments. The budget is built up from zero (i.e. no provision of service) in discreet stages representing increasing degrees of provision of service. In this way value for money can be tested as each stage builds upon the last. Furthermore, a basis is provided for a systematic selective cut back in case of need instead of a blind axe swinging exercise such as "10 percent off everybody's budget".

Management Accounting Caveats

1. *Segmental Preference*

What is the best segmental mix for a business to develop (e.g. product mix, operation mix, geographic mix)? In this and the previous two chapters we have examined techniques which should point management towards the highest operating profit via control of its two key elements: contribution and overheads. But reflect for a moment: operating management is not concerned with operating profit *per se*—operating management is ultimately concerned with RONA and cash flow from operations; contribution and overheads form part only of these two ultimate measures of performance. For example there may be no value in pushing a product mix with a high operating profit if the demands of that mix upon working capital are so huge that:

— velocity ratio is so reduced that RONA falls despite the increase in operating profit
— actual cash flow from operations becomes permanently negative.

So a good management accounting system will extend the principles described in this and the previous two chapters beyond segmental operating profit and into segmental RONA and segmental cash flow from operations.

2. *Exclusiveness*

In conclusion it must be stressed that the writer does not suggest that financial information is the only information a manager requires in order to plan, control, or reach a reasoned decision. Nor is it suggested that management accounting information can replace the manager's exercise of initiative and judgement. However, the possession of pertinent management accounting information should make easier the exercise of judgement and should help to put a price tag on any non-financial considerations.

CHAPTER 17

Capital Investment Appraisal

ARGUABLY the capital investment decision is one of the more critical that an operating manager takes in that the firm is thereby set on tramlines on which it will roll into the future and off which it may be very expensive to get. For this reason most firms justifiably put proposed capital investments under a microscope and operate rigid rules for the planning, budgeting, evaluation, control and post audit of capital expenditure. A full consideration of all aspects of such routines is beyond the scope of this book but, as part of our review of techniques of financial analysis it is appropriate briefly to review those which are applied to capital investment appraisal.

The Capital Investment Decision

Put in its simplest terms, capital investment is an exchange of values: it represents a largely irreversible outflow of cash now (capital expenditure) in exchange for a somewhat uncertain inflow of cash in the future (cash flow from operations).

Assuming that the firm wishes to be profitable, the future cash flow from operations must be big enough not only to recover the capital expenditure but to provide an adequate profit as reward for that capital investment. An adequate reward must take account of

— time: the longer one has to wait for the return, the greater the reward should be

— risk (including inflation): the greater the risk, the greater the reward should be.

Thus this simple definition of capital investment also incorporates the elements of the mechanics of capital investment appraisal, the aim of which is to ensure both recovery of the capital expenditure and the provision of an adequate reward.

Financial Information Required

The effort involved in putting together a capital investment appraisal must not be minimized. In this chapter we are concerned only with the mechanics of appraisal—which is a relatively trivial part of the whole exercise. In addition to any non-financial information which is clearly necessary, the following is a short list of the financial information which will be required in practice:

1. The initial outlay on new net operating assets (fixed assets *plus* working capital), net of the proceeds of sale of any old net operating assets being replaced.
2. Future cash flow from operations
3. The life of the project
4. Any estimated terminal values at the end of its life
5. The impact on taxation; including capital allowances, grants and subsidies
6. The timing of 1, 2, 4 and 5
7. The degree of uncertainty and key sensitivities incorporated into 1, 2, 3, 4 and 5
8. An assessment of the riskiness of the project
9. The cost of capital required to finance the project
10. In the light of all the above, the rate of return that the project should provide.

Methods of Investment Appraisal

Having accumulated this necessary financial information, it is now processed to test for the adequacy of reward. Three quite different methods of processing are found in practice:

1. *Payback*

This method ignores any reward in the form of profit from the capital expenditure and is based on after tax cash flows.

2. *RONA*

This method uses the mechanics of simple interest to test for the adequacy of reward and is based on (pre tax) operating profit.

3. DCF (Discounted Cash Flow)

This method uses the mechanics of compound interest to test for the adequacy of reward and is based on after tax cash flows. There are two variations in the use of DCF:

i. IRR (Internal Rate of Return) or DCF Yield

ii. NPV (Net Present Value) or PV (Present Value)

Let us now examine and compare the application of each of these methods to the following grossly oversimplified pair of capital investment proposals:

	Project A	Project B
	£	£
Initial capital expenditure request	£1000	£1000
Estimated future cash flow from operations in year:		
1	200	100
2	300	200
3	500	700
4	800	800
5	200	nil
Total estimated future cash flow	£2000	£1800

Assume no difference in riskiness between the two projects.
Note that project A has an estimated life of 5 years whereas B has only 4 years.

It should be glaringly obvious that project A is preferable to project B. However, let us see what each of the three methods of investment appraisal would say.

Payback Method

This is without doubt the simplest of the three and is the most widely used method in practice.

It seeks to reveal how long before the capital expenditure is repaid out of future cash inflows: in our example each project's £1000 capital expenditure is paid back in 3 years; therefore, if blindly applied, this method would rank both projects equally attractive. This would be misleading information to management because in fact A is preferable to B.

Therefore if the payback method is used, do be aware of its two weaknesses clearly demonstrated in this example:

1. it ignores that vital period *after* payback: i.e. it ignores the need to make profit
2. it fails to take account of the timing of cash flows *within* the payback period (A's timing is clearly preferable to B's).

But at least it is simple and it does concentrate on getting cash back quickly and in so doing favours the less risky project. As a safeguard against the weaknesses, some appraisal routines would quote payback against life expectancy: 3 years out of 5 for A is clearly better than 3 years out of 4 for B.

Accounting Rate of Return Method (RONA)

RONA, as we know, is operating profit expressed as a percent per annum of net operating assets (assume this is the capital expenditure only in our example). The future inflows in our example are cash flows so depreciation must be deducted in order to arrive at operating profit as follows:

Year	Project A			Project B		
	Cash flow	Dep'n 5 years	Operating profit	Cash flow	Dep'n 4 years	Operating Profit/(Loss)
	£	£	£	£	£	£
1	200	200	—	100	250	(150)
2	300	200	100	200	250	(50)
3	500	200	300	700	250	450
4	800	200	600	800	250	550
5	200	200	—	n/a	n/a	n/a
Total	2000	1000	1000	1800	1000	800
Average p.a. operating profit			200			200
Average p.a. (RONA (expressed as % initial capital expr.)			20%			20%

Based on an average p.a. RONA over the life of each project, this method has again ranked each project as equally attractive which is again misleading management information: the two projects are not equally attractive.

Therefore if the RONA method is used, do be aware of its two weaknesses clearly demonstrated here:

1. if an averaging method is used, it fails to take account of the *timing* of operating profit.

2. it is difficult to use as a basis of comparison between projects with different lives.

But at least it does give a feel for what a project might do to future RONAs if the project were to be taken on. As a safeguard against the weaknesses, some appraisal routines would average RONAs over a constant number of years, irrespective of a project's estimated life: project B clearly looks less attractive if averaged over 5 years. Furthermore, the first year's RONA ought always to be highlighted: project B's is negative.

Discounted Cash Flow Method (DCF)

In truth this method is quite simple but it rests upon more complex mathematics than the other two methods so those managers who do not have a taste for things mathematical tend to dub it "difficult".

Anyone who has a building society mortgage comes across discounted cash flow every time they make a periodic mortgage repayment; the periodic repayment is designed to do two things over the life of the mortgage:

1. repay the initial amount borrowed
2. provide a return at an agreed annual rate of compound interest on the steadily reducing outstanding balance of the amount borrowed until it is eventually repaid; the higher the rate of interest, the higher the periodic repayments—and vice versa.

Similarly, the future cash inflows from a capital project do two things:

1. repay the initial capital investment
2. provide a return at an annual compound rate on the steadily reducing outstanding balance of the investment over its useful life.

If the building society did not tell you what was the rate of compound interest implied by the size of the periodic mortgage repayments, you would have to work it out; and you would use *discount tables* (or *present value tables*) for this purpose. Similarly to work out the compound rate of return implied by the size of future cash inflows from a project you would use discount tables ... or better still a programmed calculator or micro-computer. Appendix D incorporates a discount table and brief instruction as to its use.

Internal Rate of Return

The internal rate of return (or DCF yield) *is* that compound rate of return implied by the size of future cash inflows from a project. In our example project A provides an internal rate of return of approximately 25 percent whereas project B provides approximately 20 percent. In other words both projects repay their initial capital investment but, over and above this, A provides approximately 25 percent p.a. compound return on the steadily reducing balance outstanding until repaid whereas B provides only 20 percent compound return. This statement can be proved in A's case as follows:

Year	Investment outstanding at start £ a	25% of a £ b	Cash inflow £ c	Investment outstanding at end £ d = a + b − c
1	1000	250	200	1050
2	1050	263	300	1013
3	1013	254	500	767
4	767	193	800	160
5	160	40	200	Nil
Overall	1000	1000	2000	nil

The reader is invited to carry out the same proof for project B (the return is only approximately 20 percent.

Notice that this method at last ranks project A higher than project B: the method therefore overcomes the weaknesses of the other two methods.

On the other hand the method does itself suffer from the following weaknesses:

1. The internal rate of return (being an actuarial measure based upon compound interest) does not relate to RONA (being an accounting measure based upon simple interest) therefore it fails to indicate what the project might do to the ongoing RONA of the business into which the project is to be introduced

2. It might not adequately handicap a more risky project, which the payback method would do. Take a look at project X:

Initial capital expenditure request	£1000
Estimated future cash inflows:	
years 1 to 9	nil
year 10	£20,000

The internal rate of return looks good at 35 percent but the payback does not come until year 10 of a 10 year project which is not particularly attractive and certainly is high risk ... anything can happen within the next 9 years, and probably will!

Net Present Value

A variation on the use of the discount table will tell you, for any desired compound rate of return, what is the most you ought to invest now for the right to receive a given stream of cash inflows in the future: the higher the desired rate of return, the smaller is the amount you would be prepared to invest to receive that given stream of cash inflows, and vice versa.

Suppose we require a compound rate of return of 30 percent, then the most we ought to invest in project A is £892.7, calculated as follows:

Year	Estimated future cash inflow	30% discount factor from Appendix D	Present value @ 30%
	a	b	$c = a \times b$
1	200	0.769	153.8
2	300	0.592	177.6
3	500	0.455	227.5
4	800	0.350	280.0
5	200	0.269	53.8
Total present value @ 30% of future stream of cash inflows			£ 892.7

The reader is invited to prove that the total present value @ 30 percent of the future stream of cash inflows from project B is £793.8.

Having worked out what is the most we ought to invest, we compare this to what we are asked to invest to see if we are getting a bargain. If we had been asked to invest £700 in these two projects, then project A would give the better bargain than project B: A would have a *net present value* @ 30 percent of £892.7 − £700 = £192.7 whereas B has only £93.8. So again this method ranks A higher than B.

But we were not asked to invest £700 in these projects, we were asked to invest £1000; so at that asking price A has a negative net present value of £892.7 − £1000 = − £107.3 whereas B has − £206.2: both projects are unattractive, B more so than A. Clearly a negative net present value is bad news in that it indicates that the future cash flows from a project do not promise to repay the initial capital investment *and* provide the desired compound rate of return required.

The DCF method has indicated that it is only worth going ahead with project A if your desired compound rate of return were 25 percent or with project B if your desired compound rate of return were 20 percent.

Which Appraisal Method to Use?

We have now reviewed each of the commonly used methods of capital investment appraisal. Which is best? Which one should be used?

Because *each* method suffers certain weaknesses and *each* method has certain unique advantages, the wise firm will use all three methods within its capital investment appraisal routines. After all, it represents relatively little cost and effort in the context of the whole project evaluation and might just prevent an expensive management mistake.

Ah, but what if?

No capital investment project should be appraised on one set of estimated future cash inflows alone; if any of these cash flows should turn out differently to the estimate, the project may no longer be viable. Capital investment appraisal is thus a natural for the application of sensitivity analysis and for the computation of break-even points and margins of safety. For example it would be sensible to compute the following additional information for each of our projects A and B:

1. what would happen to the financial outcome if sales were to be 10 percent lower than forecast?
2. what would happen to the financial outcome if contribution percent sales was to be X percent instead of the Y percent forecast?

... or better still:

1. by how much does sales have to fall before the project ceases to be viable?
2. by how much does contribution have to fall before the project ceases to be viable?

... and so on.

Impact of Inflation

Amongst all the uncertainties associated with estimating future cash flows, perhaps the most common is how to deal with inflation. Different firms adopt different practices and therefore it is not easy to give specific advice but the following represents a random selection of policies frequently adopted in practice:

- always estimate the impact of inflation on capital expenditures up to the date of commissioning so that the actual outlay is clearly identified
- always estimate the impact of inflation on cost reduction capital projects to highlight whether the project is viable at current spending rates or only at estimated future spending rates
- ignore the impact of inflation on future cash flows of normal revenue earning projects on the assumption that the inflationary impact on expenses will be offset by an equivalent inflationary uplift of selling prices
- carry out sensitivity tests as described above: e.g. what if inflation comes at X percent or: by how much does inflation have to move before ...?

Non Profit Earning Projects

The methods of capital investment appraisal considered in this chapter have rested on the existence of future cash inflows. But what of the project which does not offer any future cash flow, for example:

- the new machine guards required due to a change in industrial safety legislation
- the replacement central heating boiler
- the new motor car for the sales representative
- the new first aid centre
- the new word processor

These expenditures are sometimes called *lazy capital*: they provide no measurable, quantifiable, gain and so cannot be made the subject of normal capital investment appraisal routines. They can only be justified on subjective, value for money, considerations. However, often for emotional rather than economic reasons, it is very easy to indulge in such expenditures and so they must be controlled. Bear in mind that the greater the expenditure permitted on lazy capital, the greater must be the return (in RONA or IRR terms) generated on those projects which do promise a quantifiable gain: otherwise the overall RONA on total net operating assets will fall.

Is That All?

In this chapter we have looked briefly at the mechanics of capital investment appraisal. In the preamble to the chapter we observed that it was but a small part of the routines for the planning, budgeting, evaluation, control and post audit of capital expenditures. In conclusion, and for completeness, the following is a brief review of these routines to guide that reader who is interested in taking these studies further:

1. There must be some strategic and tactical direction for capital expenditures which can only come from the existence of a *long-term plan*; moreover financial planning will ensure an adequacy of financial resources to meet capital expenditures

2. There must be some formalized identification of responsibilities (coupled with spending levels) for the *authorization of capital expenditures*

3. In addition to the financial aspects of capital investment appraisal discussed in this chapter there must be adequate recognition of *non-financial aspects*: technological, personnel, production, marketing etc.

4. There must be some basis for the assessment of priorities and the *allocation of funds* in case there are competing claims for a limited supply of resources

5. There must be some formalized system for the *measurement of progress* of projects which have been authorized in order to flag up overspends or time overruns

6. Finally, the proof of the pudding being in the eating, there must be some formal system of back check, or *post audit*, some time after the project's completion in order to compare actual experience with that estimated at the time of project submission; the purpose of this being to learn from any mistake and prevent its being repeated on future projects.

CHAPTER 18

Data Processing

BOTH financial and management accounting routines require laborious, repetitive, detailed, clerical processing of data. Many thousand double entries must be made; frequent summary, addition and balancing of figures are all necessary; wages must be paid, customers billed, creditors' accounts settled: all these operations require the preparation and processing of figures and documents with speed and accuracy. Much of the work is regular but a large part revolves in weekly, monthly or annual cycles and consequently clerical routines suffer from peak periods of strain.

This type of situation obviously calls for the elimination of human drudgery by the application of mechanized aids or full automation. Mechanization and automation have been accepted as a necessary part of efficient production routines for many years and it is logical that these techniques should also be applied to the office.

In this chapter no attempt will be made to describe the various pieces of equipment available or detailed methods of operation. Equipment is constantly being modified and improved and any detailed description would quickly become out of date. If the reader desires further details he is recommended to read any of the special works which have been published on the subject or, alternatively, equipment manufacturers publish illustrated booklets and pamphlets free of charge and are only too pleased to help anyone further their knowledge of data processing techniques.

The object of this chapter simply is to introduce the reader to the main types of equipment available and to help appreciate when such equipment may be employed to the best advantage.

History of Data Processing

As long ago as the seventeenth century, when inventors were attempting to develop machines which would add, subtract or calculate, the "science of mechanical calculation" was born. Blaise Pascal invented a simple adding machine in 1642, the earliest recorded development in this field, and in 1672 Liebniz, a philosopher like Pascal, produced a primitive multiplying machine.

Great Britain entered the field in 1775 when Viscount Mahon devised an improved machine capable of multiplication and division, but the monumental, if ineffective, British contribution was Charles Babbage's "Difference Engine". Babbage had the laudable idea of developing a machine which would calculate and then print the answer. In 1823 he started work on his invention, and obtained government financial support, but the project was abandoned 10 years later, having produced nothing.

Commercial development did not come until the late nineteenth and early twentieth centuries when men whose names became household words in this field first made their contribution: Halcom Ellis, Willgodt Odhner, William Seward Burroughs, Dr. Herman Hollerith, to name a few.

A feature in the development of accounting machines was the use of electricity to replace manual operation, but a much more far-reaching change, amounting to a revolution, came about through electronics and the commercial development of the computer. Accounting machines traditionally performed their tasks by the operation of moving parts until the advent of electronics, when moving parts were no longer required. Electronics has therefore opened up the field afresh: whereas a job performed manually and counted in man-days was reduced to hours by mechanized means, it is now reduced to minutes or even seconds electronically.

The main types of equipment will now be considered. The reader may detect a theme of technical development running from one type to the next, but each type is best suited to a particular operation and it is not unusual for a firm to employ more than one type, or indeed all types, simultaneously.

"One Write" Systems

The simplest way to eliminate repetitive transcription is to employ carbon paper or carbonless copying paper. There are a number of patented "one write" systems which enable entries to be made in several records simultaneously by the careful design of multi-part stationery sets. Moreover, useful statistical analyses and summaries are produced thereby as an automatic biproduct of the system. Data processing does not necessarily imply computerization!

But let us now consider automation of accounting routines.

Adding—Calculating Machines

Originally adding machines accumulated figures on dials on the same principle as a clock or gas meter, but eventually accumulation was on revolving counters as mileage is accumulated in a car. The best-known adding machine type was the Comptometer, whereby the depression of an appropriate key activated the revolving counters by a desired amount. Multiplication and division are in fact mass addition and subtraction and so the Comptometer became also a calculating machine by the repetitive depression of keys.

A calculating machine proper, by incorporating special mechanisms and a moving carriage, eliminated the need for repetitive depression of keys; after a single depression the calculation continued automatically, thus reducing the possibility of operator error. The answer to a calculation was read off from the revolving counters, but some machines incorporated a print unit, and, in this case, the answer was printed out on a narrow roll of paper, or "till roll", attached to the machine. This type of machine was referred to as an add/listing or calculating/listing machine.

Electronics has eliminated the need for moving parts and modern electronic calculations are much smaller and compact. Answers to calculations appear on a visual display panel but some do also incorporate small till rolls.

Keyboard Accounting Machines

These machines combined the principles of calculating machines and typewriters and were therefore fitted with a complete typewriter keyboard (augmented by special keys to cause the printing of certain repetitive information automatically) in addition to the figure keyboard of the calculating machine. Capabilities of individual machines varied widely, depending on their size and construction, but generally speaking they carried out a book-keeping sequence, completing all necessary documentation, calculations and figurework in the one operation. An important feature of these machines was their automatic "proof", or check of accuracy, on all parts of the arithmetical routines carried out. Again these machines underwent a minor revolution with the advent of electronics.

Receipt Analysis Machines

These machines specialized in the control of incoming revenue by the simultaneous production of a printed receipt, a detailed statistical analysis and occasionally the entry in a permanent account or pass book. Developed from the cash register, such machines were often used to record receipts in local authority rating offices, gas and electricity boards offices and savings banks. With the additional benefit of a computer link up, such machines became capable of much greater analysis and found application much more widely throughout retailing and banking.

Punched-card Equipment

All the above types of equipment worked on the basic principle of manual depression of a key which activated the mechanism of the machine, but punched-card equipment worked on an entirely different principle. Cards having holes punched in them were stacked in an automatic feed hopper of the machine and the hole in the card activated the mechanism.

Basic data from original sources of information were translated into a series of punched holes in card records, the accuracy of the punching was then verified and the card became an accurate permanent record of a transaction, available for processing in any way desired. Cards were sorted into any predetermined sequence before being fed into the tabulator, which printed selected information in accordance with prior instructions of the operator. The cards were then available for re-sorting again and again to produce further selected information. The technique was developed by Dr. Herman Hollerith and used in connection with the U.S.A. census of population of 1890; it was particularly applicable to the processing of data requiring a high degree of statistical analysis.

A basic punched-card installation comprised a punch, verifier, sorter and tabulator but other items of equipment could be added to perform special tasks as required, e.g. multiplication or interpretation of holes into printed characters.

Computers

Brief reference to computers was made in earlier sections, the main development over other mechanized aids being the substitution of electronic circuits for moving parts. Subsequent developments in computer technology have been rapid and equipment tends to become obsolete rather quickly. One of the more significant "revolutions" was the commercial development of the silicon chip, thereby creating even further potential for micro-miniaturization. Computer power has tended to increase as computer size and cost have reduced.

Two attributes distinguish the computer from any other type of equipment discussed above: speed and memory. A computer performs its tasks with lightning speed and thus makes possible the production of information previously thought impossible due to factors of time and clerical cost. A computer's memory consists of information transcribed usually on to magnetic tape or disc; rapid access to the memory permits the computer to up-date information, make comparisons or test for accuracy at the same lightning speed; moreover the memory is not retained in hard copy form.

A basic computer installation comprises the following five units: input (usually magnetic tape, punched paper tape or keyboard), memory, arithmetic (performs the calculations), output (rapid printing) and control (supervises the accuracy of other units).

Microcomputer Modelling

Perhaps the most revolutionary development to hit the accounting profession in recent history has been the combination of microcomputer and spreadsheet modelling. The spreadsheet model is equivalent to a vast sheet of analysis paper, many many columns wide and many many lines deep: the answer to a financial analyst's prayer! Almost any amount of analysis can be done with incredible speed and on a highly portable machine—so it can be done anywhere. Moreover, all aspects of budgeting and planning are aided by the ability to test several possible alternative scenarios, answer "what if" questions, highlight critical limiting factors and margins of safety: a facility called *sensitivity analysis*.

Three examples crying out for such applications can be selected from the various financial analysis techniques discussed in this book:

— the hard graft of financial ratio analysis described in Chapter 11 and culminating in the financial fault finding chart described in Chapter 12
— the tedious calculations required for cost rate computation described in Chapter 14
— the sensitivity tests and detailed calculations demanded by capital investment appraisal referred to in Chapter 17.

What to Automate

Any aspect of accounting routines can be automated singly (e.g. payroll, sales ledger, stores records) by employing the appropriate type of equipment; alternatively, complete data-processing routines may be automated: E.D.P. or *electronic data processing* is the name given to this complete processing by computer.

Related Developments

An interesting adjunct to the march of automation has been the development of forms, books and equipment for use with the machines:

1. Traditional forms of ledger, account, invoice, statement, cheque and receipt, for example, have been thrown aside as a new art of *form design* has grown up. Modern forms must conveniently fit the machine and information contained in the form must be set out for ease of machine application. A series of forms, accounts and statistical summaries is now produced in one operation, by means of carbon or other process, therefore size and ruling must be co-ordinated to ensure correct register on all parts of the series.

2. Machines best operate continuously and so the use of *continuous stationery* has increased: forms are run together in a continuous stream and later separated along perforated joints.

3. *Security* assumes greater importance when systems are no longer designed around bound books (which cannot fit into a machine) but around a loose leaf or a magnetic tape or disk. Filing systems, lockable trays, and other special office furniture and equipment have therefore developed apace.

4. Much information is no longer kept in hard copy form but is retained within the computer. *Information transmission* through visual display units (VDUs) and telephonic transfer has therefore been developed.

Why Automate?

Advantages of automated over hand-written systems are considerable; some of the more obvious are listed below. The degree of importance attaching to each item on the list depends upon the particular requirements of each firm and no order of priority is intended in the alphabetical presentation adopted.

1. *Accuracy* is improved because automated systems incorporate their own checks or "proof" of accuracy *after each entry*. Chapter 2 described the proof of arithmetical accuracy laboriously provided over a hand-written system by the trial balance.

2. *Duplication* of effort is minimized because automated systems simultaneously enter all figures and prepare all documents which, under a hand-written system, constitute a series of transcriptive operations. For example, a mechanized payroll routine produces payroll, pay advice, tax deduction card, envelope and statistical analysis in one operation. Further advantages arising are the economy of manpower and the elimination of cyclical peak periods such as periodic balancing and summarizing, or preparation of statements to send to customers.

3. *Information* is produced more quickly and conveniently, often as a by-product at no extra effort (as in payroll analysis under 2 above). Certain information may be made available which could not possibly be obtained by hand.

4. *Security* is improved, when all entries are made by machine as part of an integrated system, and fraud becomes more difficult to perpetrate.

5. *Simplicity*. An intricate clerical task, which only a skilled clerk can perform manually, may be converted to a machine program. It then becomes a simple machine operation that a trained operator can perform with ease by depressing the appropriate keys. Training of an operator is training in machine operation, not in intricate clerical duties.

6. *Speed* is a feature of automation: speed in preparing information and in rendering accounts to customers are two examples vital to managerial control.

Advantages of automation are often used as an ill-judged argument for crashing into systems without counting the cost. The final section of this chapter is therefore devoted to some dangers which must be considered before embarking upon a scheme of automation.

Dangers of Automation

A scheme of automation is a costly investment which should not be undertaken lightly. Financial justification may prove difficult because it is difficult to put a price tag on certain of the advantages to be gained—how valuable is information, for example? However, two exercises should be carried out: firstly, the financial commitment should be accurately assessed and secondly certain non-financial questions should be answered.

Is the equipment to be purchased outright or hired? This part of the financial commitment is clear, but it is only a part because other facilities may be required which also form part of the cost: space, power, lighting and ventilation must be adequate for the machines, ancillary equipment or alterations in form design, records and filing systems may be necessary; qualified staff may be required to run the installation. Every aspect of the proposed change must be investigated to ensure that there is no expensive hidden item and, when the total commitment has been ascertained, the question must be asked, "Will we get value for our money?"

Non-financial matters must be headed by a clear statement of the reason for wishing to automate in this way. Is this the best machine for the job, selected after due consideration of all available alternatives and after discounting over-ambitious "sales talk"—or is the machine desired for prestige or because it is the done thing? Will this machine link in with existing machines or otherwise be capable of tackling additional jobs as occasion demands—or is it a special-purpose inflexible machine which may never be fully employed and may soon become obsolete?

There must never be mere automation of existing clerical routines: need and method must be justified, by organization and methods investigation, to ensure the most efficient method of data processing. This investigation may be provided as part of the service by the equipment distributor.

Have staff problems been adequately considered? Existing staff may not be good material for retraining from pen to machine, although, if they are, the equipment distributor often provides training again as part of the service. If retraining is not practicable the two-headed problem of dealing with redundant staff and acquiring suitable new staff is raised.

Finally the extent to which the machine is to be used must be considered. No machine is cheap, but computer installations in particular may run into many tens or hundreds of thousands of pounds. The comments on importance of volume made in Chapter 15 have their implication here also: if value for money is to be obtained, the machines must be worked to the full and the maximum possible benefit extracted. To this end it is advisable to have in charge of an expensive installation a skilled technician who appreciates what the machines can and cannot do and also what information management requires. Only in this way will an installation be operated as efficiently and economically as possible and be of maximum benefit to management in its pursuit of financial viability.

CHAPTER 19

Principles of Corporate Taxation

NOTE: The rates of tax and allowances quoted in this chapter are those in force at the time of writing except where stated to the contrary.

NO VOLUME of this size could deal fully with the subject of corporate taxation but an elementary appreciation of its principles is necessary for two reasons: first, there is a tremendous display of ignorance generally about the simple fundamentals of taxation, and second, most business management decisions can only be taken after seriously considering the possible effect of taxation.

The subjects of personal taxation, value added tax, capital gains tax and inheritance tax are considered to be beyond the scope of this book and so are not considered.

Tax Legislation

Taxation is a device for raising public revenue and is based on an accumulating body of legislation which is added to and amended from time to time as particular needs, crises and political manœuvres demand. Whereas most laws are drafted to solve the problems arising from an existing set of circumstances, tax laws often must be drafted to deal with circumstances which have not yet arisen. Tax laws therefore must first clearly define certain anticipated circumstances and then indicate precisely how they are to be dealt with. Such a body of legislation cannot permit of "equitable interpretation" or "fair play" or "the spirit of the thing": the letter of the law is absolute and final until amended by further Act of Parliament. Many manifestations of taxation legislation may appear anomalous or unjust to the reader—the fact that they are nevertheless correct stems from the letter of the law. To repeat: the letter of tax law is absolute and final; accept this fact, try not to reason with it and an understanding of the implications of tax legislation will be the more easy.

An important corollary to this fact is that if one's affairs can be so arranged as to fall outside the letter of the law, tax will be avoided. Many accountants, lawyers and others therefore expend great effort in minimizing their client's tax liability—all quite legal. Legal avoidance of tax becomes quite a game: the legislature closes the loopholes so the taxpayer seeks out new ones through which to avoid tax, but these will be closed by the legislature if exploited too far so the taxpayer seeks out new ones again! And so it goes on—a game of leapfrog with the obstacles becoming more and more difficult as time passes by.

Avoidance must not be confused with evasion, which is fraudulently escaping one's legal liability to tax—for example, by making false statements to the authorities. Avoidance is quite legal: evasion is illegal.

Administration

Parliament is primarily responsible for control over public revenue although the administration of public finance is carried out by the Treasury, which includes amongst its members the Chancellor of the Exchequer.

Administration of tax legislation is vested in a group of permanent civil servants who constitute the Board of Inland Revenue. The Board in turn appoint Commissioners of Taxes (who deal with assessments to tax, appeals and any other special matters) and Inspectors of Taxes (who agree the liability to tax of all taxpayers within their geographical area or "tax district").

Actual collection of money is the responsibility of the Collectors of Taxes for each area.

Corporation Tax

The tax on profits of limited companies and certain other corporate bodies is called Corporation Tax. The rate is fixed annually by the Finance Act: currently (1993) the rate is 33 percent although there is relief for companies with profits of under £100,000.

Taxable Profits

Corporation Tax is not necessarily calculated on the profit before taxation appearing in the company's profit and loss account. It is calculated on the company's *statutory income* or *taxable profit*: to the profit before taxation are added certain items which the accumulation of tax legislation dictates shall not be allowed as a deduction from profits for tax purposes but similarly certain deductions are made which perhaps had not been taken into account in arriving at the company's profit before taxation.

What shall and shall not be allowed as a deduction in computing statutory income is a subject in itself but, generally speaking, anything which smacks of capital expenditure or represents an element of improvement in the assets of a business is disallowed; any other expense is allowed provided that it is wholly and exclusively for business purposes—needless to say business entertaining expenses come under very close scrutiny by the Inspector of Taxes.

A major adjustment in the computation of statutory income is capital allowances so this is considered in some detail below.

Capital Allowances

Depreciation as such is not an allowable deduction in arriving at statutory income and therefore will be added back to profit before taxation in the tax computation. However, tax legislation permits instead the deduction of *capital allowances* which have the same basic object as depreciation but are also designed to operate as tax incentives to reinvestment and as a primitive hedge against inflation.

It is because capital allowances are designed partially as a tax incentive to reinvestment that the exact basis of their calculation changes frequently as economic and political pressures come to bear on the government of the day: sometimes a large first year allowance followed by smaller annual writing down allowances have been given; there have been times when the first year allowance was 100 percent for certain approved expenditures on fixed assets. At the time of writing (1993) the following is a brief summary of the position:

1. there is no large first year allowance
2. approved expenditure on plant, machinery and vehicles qualifies for an annual writing down allowance of 25 percent calculated on the reducing balance method
3. expenditure on new agricultural and industrial buildings and hotels qualifies for an annual writing down allowance of 4 percent calculated on the straight line method
4. no allowance is given on non-industrial buildings

5. higher rates of allowance might be given on assets employed in enterprise zones
6. an adjustment may be necessary when an asset is disposed of at the end of its life.

Capital allowances are given as a deduction in arriving at taxable profits as demonstrated in the simple example below. Unlike government grants, they have no immediate cash value. Their ultimate cash value is in the corporation tax that the company is shielded from paying by reason of this deduction from profits which would otherwise be taxed.

Here is a very simple demonstration of how taxable profits are computed; the main message of the demonstration is that taxable profits are likely to be different in amount to the profits before taxation which appear in the profit and loss account:

	£
Profit before taxation, as in the profit and loss account	200
Add back depreciation charged in arriving at profit before taxation	70
	270
Deduct capital allowances	100
Taxable profit for the year	170
Deduct unrelieved tax losses brought forward	70
Net assessable profits for tax purposes	£ 100
Corporation tax payable thereon @ 33%	£ 33

The £33 is called *Mainstream Corporation Tax* and will be referred to again shortly.

Tax Losses

If, after going through the computation of statutory income, a company reveals a loss for tax purposes this may be carried back 1 year and a claim made for repayment of any mainstream corporation tax paid in that year. Any part of the taxable loss still unrelieved may then be carried forward indefinitely to set off against future profits arising in the same business as demonstrated above.

Payment of Corporation Tax

Corporation tax is payable in two stages:

1. Mainstream Corporation Tax is due and payable 9 months after the end of the company's financial year in which the assessable profits arose

This generous credit by the government is clearly advantageous to cash flow; however, it is a two-edged sword because it also means that the cash value of capital allowances are not felt until 9 months after the year in which they have been earned.

2. However, a significant acceleration of the date of payment of corporation tax might occur due to the incidence of Advance Corporation Tax which we must next explore.

Advance Corporation Tax (ACT)

When a company pays a dividend to shareholders it is deemed, for tax purposes, to be paid after deduction of personal income tax at the basic personal rate, currently (1993) 20 percent. Thus if a company paid a dividend of £80 the tax authorities would deem this to be £100 less £20 *imputed* personal income tax. This imputed tax clearly is calculated at $20/80 \times$ the dividend paid and is called Advanced Corporation Tax or ACT.

The imputed amount must be paid over to the Collector of Taxes within 2 weeks of the end of the quarter during which the dividend was paid. Any such payments are deemed to be on account of, and hence can be deducted from, the next payment of mainstream corporation tax liability. Hence the title *Advance* Corporation Tax.

For example: assume that the company in the simple demonstration on page 190 decided to pay a dividend of £80—this will give rise to an ACT payment of $20/80 \times £80$, or £20 and hence the corporation tax payment pattern will be as follows:

		£
ACT paid within 2 weeks of the end of the quarter in which the dividend is paid		20
Mainstream liability paid 9 months after the financial year end	33	
deduct ACT payment	20	13
Total corporation tax payable		£ 33

But ACT is in effect the "Catch 22" of capital allowances and loss relief! Suppose that, in the simple demonstration on page 190, the company had unrelieved tax losses brought forward of £150: its net assessable profits for tax purposes would be only £20 and its mainstream liability thereon @ 33 percent would be £7. But if the company still pays a dividend of £80 (after all it does have a profit before taxation this year of £200) then it must still make an ACT payment of £20 which it can deduct from its next mainstream liability . . . of £7. So the company has overpaid £13; this will not be repaid but is called *unrecovered ACT* and may be carried forward indefinitely until such time as it has an adequate mainstream liability from which to make the deduction. But what if it has another low mainstream liability next year? Many companies have found themselves in the unfortunate position of accumulating a "mountain" of unrecovered ACT:

— the good news is that they will have relatively little mainstream corporation tax to pay in the foreseeable future
— the bad news is that the unrecovered ACT has created an unfortunate drain on its cash flow
— the other bad news is that future legislation could possibly impose a time limit on the carry forward of unrelieved ACT

U.K. based multinational companies earning a relatively large proportion of their profits overseas and a relatively small proportion in the U.K. have also accumulated a mountain of unrecovered ACT. Dividends paid in the U.K. trigger off the ACT payment which can only be deducted from future *U.K.* mainstream liability—it cannot be deducted from overseas tax liabilities. So if a U.K. multinational pays a dividend to its U.K. shareholders based on its *world wide* profits it could very easily trigger off an ACT payment which is substantially higher than the mainstream liability arising from its *U.K.* taxable profits.

Several companies have offered shareholders additional shares in lieu of a cash dividend in order to avoid the payment of ACT and so prevent adding to their mountain of unrecovered ACT. (ACT is only payable on a *cash* distribution to shareholders.)

Deferred Taxation

From earlier sections of this chapter it will be apparent that the payment for corporation tax in any year may bear little relationship to 33 percent of the profit before taxation which appears in the company's profit and loss account for that year. However these two amounts should approximate to each other over time because any difference arises largely due to timing; an obvious example is the difference between the rate at which capital expenditure is spread via depreciation compared to how it is spread via capital allowances—over the whole life of the asset the two amounts must be the same in total.

Applying the accounting concept of relevance (see page 29), these timing differences can be ironed out through the technique of adjusting for deferred taxation. Let us return again to our demonstration on page 190, but, for simplicity, assume that there are no unrelieved tax losses brought forward: 33 percent of the profit before taxation of £200 is £66 yet the corporation tax payable would be only £56.1 (33 percent of the taxable profit of £170). The difference of £9.9 is explained by the difference between depreciation (£70) and capital allowances (£100) or £30 @ 33 percent. To iron out this difference, an entry in the profit and loss account might appear as follows:

		£
Profit before taxation		200
Taxation:		
U.K. corporation tax @ 33%	56.1	
Deferred taxation	9.9	66
Profit after taxation		134

The £9.9 will be shown as deferred taxation in the balance sheet under provision for liabilities and charges (see for example page 207 for Typical Products Ltd.). This balance sheet entry will accumulate over the years and subsequently, if capital allowances are lower than the depreciation charge, an appropriate amount will be transferred back from deferred taxation to the profit and loss account. Hence the adjustment for deferred taxation irons out any timing differences so that the charge for corporation tax appears in the profit and loss account at the amount which would have been payable had the company's depreciation charge been allowed as capital allowances.

Deferred taxation can be more complicated than this in practice (see for example note 6 to John Waddington PLC's accounts at page 220).

In practice a provision for deferred taxation will only be made to the extent that the directors of the company feel that there is a reasonable probability of its having to be paid in the foreseeable future.

Taxation and Management Decisions

Management is constantly being called upon to take decisions. The financial implication of a proposed course of action is one of the matters to be weighed in the balance when reaching a decision. The assistance which can be given to management by financial and management accounting has been discussed in earlier chapters; however, the financial result of any course of action must take into account the effect of taxation and this matter must never be overlooked if a reasoned decision is to be taken.

Some of the questions which might be asked are:

1. Will any contemplated expenditure be allowed as a deduction from income in computing taxable profit for Corporation Tax purposes?

2. If disallowed, may it be regarded as capital expenditure and so be available for capital allowances?

3. Irrespective of the answer to 1 and 2, can a government grant be claimed?

4. Is the timing to the best advantage? This is important, apart from ACT, because tax legislation and rates of tax change over a period of time.

5. Have affairs been arranged, documents been worded and events been followed to the best tax advantage, bearing in mind the letter of the law? Professional advice should be taken here.

An example often quoted of the effect of arrangement of affairs concerns the raising of capital. Assume that all other considerations have been dealt with and the final decision now lies between preference capital and a debenture. Corporation Tax is affected because debenture interest is an allowable deduction for Corporation Tax purposes but preference dividend is not. With Corporation Tax at 33 percent, it becomes much more expensive to service a preference dividend than debenture interest of the same amount:

	10% Debenture	10% Preference
	£	£
Operating profit	300	300
Interest payable on debenture	60	—
Profit before taxation	240	300
Corporation tax @ 33%	79	99
Profit after taxation	161	201
Preference dividend	—	60
Profit attributable to ordinary shareholders	£161	£141

Note that ordinary shareholders are better off by £20 under the debenture alternative. This is the benefit from tax shield on debenture interest (33 percent of £60), i.e. the amount of tax which the company is shielded from paying by nature of the tax deductibility of debenture interest if the decision is made in this way.

Mr. Bumble, in *Oliver Twist*, said that "The law is a ass". Perhaps this is not true of all law, but tax law certainly can appear to be at times.

Conclusion and Summary

THIS BOOK has been built on the premise that the prime *financial* purpose of any business is the pursuit of two financial objectives:

1. To make a profit over the long-term adequate to remunerate the investment made in that business.

2. To generate a cash flow adequate to ensure continuing economic survival of that business.

The reader has been introduced to various aspects of business accounting and to their inherent limitations. Interpretation of accounts has been a major feature and the view of accounting as a service to management has also been stressed.

That accounting is an indispensable aid to efficient business management cannot be doubted: a vital factor when pursuing economic goals is sound financial management, guided by information produced by the accounting service.

But what is accounting trying to measure, what are the financial flows around the business and what is the interrelationship between the many terms used in accounting reports? Perhaps it would be useful to summarize and pull together much of what has been discussed piecemeal through the 19 chapters of this book. The flow chart appearing on page 197 attempts to do this and should be looked at in the light of the following commentary.

1. The six rectangles across the chart represent the essential elements of any business: i.e. we need customers, assets, suppliers, employees, providers of capital . . . and government. Notice that there are two types of net operating assets and two types of providers of capital.

2. The business cycle begins at the left of the chart when the customer places an order which is then processed through the utilization of fixed assets and working capital to produce sales.

3. From sales is deducted direct costs which leaves contribution and from this is next deducted indirect materials and indirect labour to leave potential cash flow from operations, or PCFO.

Financial structure of a business

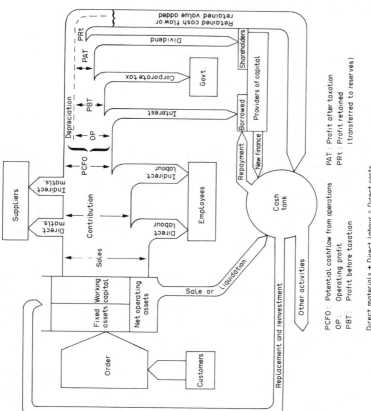

PCFO : Potential cashflow from operations
OP : Operating profit
PBT : Profit before taxation

PAT : Profit after taxation
PRt : Profit retained
(transferred to reserves)

Direct materials + Direct labour = Direct costs

Indirect materials + Indirect labour + Deprecation = Overheads

PAT ÷ no of shares = EPS (Earnings per Share)

4. PCFO now is split into two parts: depreciation and operating profit, or OP.

5. Successively, OP now remunerates those who have lent money to the business (interest), the government (corporate tax) and the shareholders (dividend) finally leaving profit retained in the business or PRt.

6. PRt plus depreciation now represent the total retention in the business which flows down and round to the cash tank.

7. Additionally the cash tank takes in new finance from the providers of capital plus any proceeds of sale or liquidation of net operating assets.

8. Management of the business now filters the available cash into one or more of four channels:

(i) repayment of borrowed money;
(ii) back into the top of the net operating asset tank, i.e. the reinvestment in existing fixed assets and working capital on a replacement basis (including to provide for inflation) to ensure continuity of the business;
(iii) again back into the top of the net operating asset tank but this time to provide for expansion of the existing business
(iv) movement into the net operating asset tank of some other activity or into non-operating assets . . . and so on round and round.

But observe

9. If the total retention in the business from 6 above becomes smaller, either because sales are too small or because any of the expenses between sales and profit retained are too great, it may become difficult to ensure an adequacy of finance for expansion, or even for replacement: a business must generate retentions to survive.

10. In times of inflation, more and more cash must be pumped from the cash tank into the top of the net operating asset tank just to provide for increased cost of replacement; this therefore requires a greater input of cash into the tank just to stand still or alternatively it may prevent real expansion and/or investment in other activities.

Accounting is not a device for pulling management out of a hopeless situation. A critical financial situation does not develop overnight: debtors do not suddenly cease to pay, stocks do not accumulate within the hour, creditors do not all clamour for payment without due warning, equipment does not suddenly require replacement, profits do not become losses without warning—all these things take place gradually over a period of time. It is too late for financial management when the position has become hopeless!

Accounting information, for all its weaknesses and imperfections, will give adequate warning of unfavourable trends if frequently prepared and intelligently applied. Remedial action can then be taken whilst there is yet time and the health of the business preserved for the future. Small doses of remedial action are much easier to administer, and take effect much more quickly, than a large-scale last ditch rescue operation. If a business is to be successful, its management must subscribe to the proverb "an ounce of prevention is worth a pound of cure".

Summary of Provisions of Companies Acts 1985 and 1989 re Disclosure in Published Accounts of Limited Companies

General

With certain exemptions for small and medium sized companies (see below), every company shall, once at least in every calendar year, lay before the company in general meeting a profit and loss account and balance sheet containing the detailed particulars required by the Companies Acts.

These financial statements must give a true and fair view of the company's state of affairs and must be compiled by applying the four fundamental accounting concepts discussed in Chapter 4 at page 29. Either historical cost accounting rules (either with or without revaluations of property) or current cost accounting rules may be applied.

The 1981 Act, in compliance with the Fourth Directive of the EC, introduced for the first time rigid formats for financial satements which are confirmed by the 1985 Act and described below. The statements may be put together in either horizontal or vertical form (see pages 24 and 25 for a description of these two methods) but must disclose the principal captions identified below by letters and roman numerals. Subsidiary captions, identified by arabic numerals, may be combined together, or relegated to notes for convenience, or omitted altogether if immaterial.

Balance Sheet Format

Format 1 uses the vertical, or net assets approach whilst Format 2 uses the horizontal, or total assets approach. However, both must contain the following information:

Assets

A. Called up share capital not paid (alternatively can be shown at C II 5)
B. Fixed assets
   I Intangible assets
      1. Development costs
      2. Concessions, patents, licences, trade marks and similar rights and assets
      3. Goodwill (to the extent that it was acquired for valuable consideration)
      4. Payments on account
   II Tangible assets
      1. Land and buildings
      2. Plant and machinery
      3. Fixtures, fittings, tools and equipment
      4. Payments on account and assets in course of construction
   III Investments
      1. Shares in group companies
      2. Loans to group companies
      3. Shares in related companies
      4. Loans to related companies
      5. Other investments other than loans
      6. Other loans
      7. Own shares
C. Current assets
   I Stocks
      1. Raw materials and consumables
      2. Work in progress
      3. Finished goods and goods for resale
      4. Payments on account
   II Debtors (amounts falling due within one year to be shown separately from amounts falling due after more than one year)
      1. Trade debtors
      2. Amounts owed by group companies
      3. Amounts owed by related companies
      4. Other debtors
      5. Called up share capital not paid (alternatively can be shown at A)

     6. Prepayments and accrued income (alternatively can be shown at D)
- III Investments
  - 1. Shares in group companies
  - 2. Own shares
  - 3. Other investments
- IV Cash at bank and in hand

D. Prepayments and accrued income (alternatively can be shown at C II 6)

Liabilities

A. Capital and reserves
- I Called up share capital
- II Share premium account
- III Revaluation reserve
- IV Other reserves
  - I. Capital redemption reserve
  - 2. Reserve for own shares
  - 3. Reserves provided for by the articles of association
  - 4. Other reserves
- V Profit and loss account

B. Provisions for liabilities and charges
- 1. Pensions and similar obligations
- 2. Taxation including deferred taxation
- 3. Other provisions

C. Creditors (amounts falling due within one year to be shown separately from amounts falling due after more than one year)
- 1. Debenture loans (convertible loans to be shown separately)
- 2. Bank loans and overdrafts
- 3. Payments received on account
- 4. Trade creditors
- 5. Bills of Exchange payable
- 6. Amounts owed to group companies
- 7. Amounts owed to related companies
- 8. Other creditors including taxation and social security
- 9. Accruals and deferred income (alternatively can be shown at D)

D. Accruals and deferred income (alternatively can be shown at C 9)

Profit and Loss Account Format

Formats 1 and 2 use the vertical approach whilst Formats 3 and 4 use the horizontal approach. Two alternative approaches to content are permissible as demonstrated below:

Formats 1 and 3 must contain the following information (note that all items are identified by arabic numerals—see comment above):

1. Turnover
2. Cost of sales
3. Gross profit or loss
4. Distribution costs
5. Administrative expenses
6. Other operating income
7. Income from shares in group companies
8. Income from shares in related companies
9. Income from other fixed asset investments
10. Other interest receivable and similar income
11. Amounts written off investments
12. Interest payable and similar charges
13. Tax on profit or loss on ordinary activities
14. Profit or loss on ordinary activities after taxation
15. Extraordinary income
16. Extraordinary charges
17. Extraordinary profit or loss
18. Tax on extraordinary profit or loss
19. Other taxes not shown under the above items
20. Profit or loss for the financial year

Expense analysis in Formats 1 and 3 is classified by function as in items 2, 4 and 5 above. Formats 2 and 4 owe much to the Value Added Statement concept and so classify expense by type, e.g. materials, staff costs, depreciation. In Formats 2 and 4 the following information must be given instead of items 2 to 5 above:

change in stocks of finished goods and work in progress
own work capitalized
raw materials and consumables
other external charges
staff costs:
  (a) wages and salaries
  (b) social security costs

(c) other pension costs
depreciation and other amounts written off fixed assets
exceptional amounts written off current assets
other operating charges

An analysis of turnover and profit before taxation shall be given for each significantly different class of business carried on and an analysis of turnover by different markets shall also be given.

If Formats 1 or 3 are selected, the amount of any provision for depreciation shall be shown by way of note.

Particulars to be disclosed in Directors' Report

In addition to certain domestic matters (e.g. names of directors, principal activities of the group, dividend recommendation) the report shall give a fair review of the development of the business of the company and its subsidiaries during the year and of their position at the end of it. It shall also give the following specific information:

(a) important post balance sheet events
(b) likely future developments
(c) research and development activities
(d) charitable and political contributions.

Small and Medium Sized Companies

The Fourth Directive of the EC defined a small and medium sized company in terms of European Units of Account which may be revised from time to time. The Act follows the Fourth Directive and defines a small and medium sized company as one which meets two out of three of the following criteria: (The values for the first two criteria are current at the time of writing—1993)

	Small	*Medium*
Turnover not exceeding	£2 million	£8 million
Total assets not exceeding	£975 thousand	£3.9 million
Number of employees not exceeding	50	250

Small companies need only file an abbreviated balance sheet and need not file either a profit and loss account or a directors' report.

Medium sized companies need not disclose details or analysis of turnover nor cost of sales nor other operating income.

Extracts from the Published Accounts Booklet of Typical Products Ltd.

Notes:

1. These accounts are quite hypothetical and are presented as support material to Chapters 6, 11 and 12.

2. Expressions used in these accounts are explained in Chapter 6, pages 56–57.

3. The interpretation of financial information contained in these accounts is explained in Chapter 11, pages 97–110 and Chapter 12, page 116.

4. Appendix C is an actual extract from the published accounts booklet of John Waddingon PLC for the year ended 3 April 1993. The reader may find it interesting to compare this with the hypothetical extract contained in Appendix B.

Typical Products Ltd. and Subsidiary Companies
Consolidated Profit and Loss Account for the year ended . . .

Last yr. £000s		See note	This yr. £000s
2,025	Sales (or turnover)	1	3,500
123	Operating profit	2	168
6	Interest payable		26
117	Profit on ordinary activities before taxation		142
51	Taxation	3	58
66	Profit on ordinary activities after taxation		84
1	Attributable to minority interests in subsidiaries		2
65	Profit attributable to Typical Products Ltd. shareholders		82
3	Extraordinary items		3
62	Profit for the financial year		79
28	Dividends	4	60
£ 34	Profit retained, transferred to reserves		£ 19
26.0p	Earnings per share	5	18.2p

Statement of Retained Profits

156	Profit and loss account at end of last year		190
34	Profit retained this year		19
£ 190	Profit and loss account at end of this year		£ 209

Reconciliation of Movement in Shareholders' Funds

62	Profit for the financial year		79
28	Dividends		60
34			19
—	New share capital issued		300
34	Net addition to shareholders' funds		319
456	Shareholders' funds at end of last year		490
£490	Shareholders' funds at end of this year		£809

Typical Products Ltd. and Subsidiary Companies
Consolidated Balance Sheet as at ...

Last yr. £000s		See note	This yr. £000s
	Fixed assets		
262	Tangible assets	7	430
15	Investments		15
277			445
	Current assets		
262	Stocks and work in progress	8	703
254	Trade debtors		611
22	Cash at bank and in hand		8
538			1322
	Creditors—amounts falling due within one year		
—	Bank overdrafts		190
201	Trade creditors		613
2	Taxation payable	3	4
18	Dividend payable	4	40
221			847
317	Net current assets		475
594	Total assets less current liabilities		920
	Creditors—amounts falling due after more than one year		
50	12% Debentures 2025/2030		50
	Provision for liabilities and charges		
46	Deferred taxation	3	53
£ 498	Net assets		£ 817
	Capital and reserves		
250	Called up share capital	9	450
—	Share premium account	9 & 6	100
50	Revaluation reserve		50
190	Profit and loss account		209
490	Shareholders' funds		809
8	Minority interests in subsidiaries		8
£ 498			£ 817

Typical Products Ltd. and Subsidiary Companies
Cash Flow Statement

Last yr. £000s			See note		This yr. £000s
123		Operating profit			168
13		Depreciation	2		38
136		Potential cash flow from operations			206
		Movement in fixed assets	7		
	10	Sale		23	
	(40)	Purchase		(229)	
(30)					(206)
		Movement in working capital			
	(30)	Stocks (increase)/decrease		(441)	
	(25)	Trade debtors (increase)/decrease		(357)	
	52	Trade creditors (decrease)/increase		412	
(3)					(386)
103		Actual cash flow from operations			(386)
		Non-operating cash flows			
(55)		Taxation paid	3		(49)
		Financial obligation			
(6)		Interest paid			(26)
(26)		Dividend paid	4		(38)
(1)		Profit attributable to minority interests			(2)
(3)		Extraordinary items			(3)
—		Issue of new ordinary shares	9		300
12		Total cash flow for the year			(204)
(40)		Cash at bank and in hand/(net borrowing) at beginning of the year			(28)
£(28)		Cash at bank and in hand/(net borrowing) at the end of the year*			£(232)
		* Net borrowing at end of year:			
22		Cash at bank and in hand			8
—		Bank overdrafts			(190)
(50)		Debentures			(50)
£(28)					£(232)

Typical Products Ltd. and Subsidiary Companies
Notes supporting the accounts for the year ended ...

Please Note:

These notes are reproduced only to assist the financial analysis of the accounts. They do not purport to reflect the Notes to the Accounts which must be incorporated in published accounts booklets to fulfil legal and other requirements. In practice the Notes to the Accounts are both detailed and lengthy; the example from John Waddington PLC at pages 216 to 228 is a good reflection of best current practice.

Last yr. £000s				This yr. £000s
2025	1. Sales			3500
	This represents amounts invoiced to external customers excluding VAT (Value Added Tax)			
	2. Operating profit			
13	This is after charging depreciation of			38
	3. Taxation			
51	a. The charge in the profit and loss account is the relevant charge for the year and includes an element of deferred taxation (see page 193)			58
	b. The actual payment in the cash flow statement is made up as follows:			
	Amount owing at start of year (see balance sheet)			
	Taxation payable		2	
52	Deferred taxation		46	48
51	Add the charge from the profit and loss acount			58
103				106
	Deduct amount owing at end of year			
2	Taxation payable		4	
46	Deferred taxation		53	
48				57
55	Equals taxation paid (see cash flow statement)			49
	4. Dividends			
	a. the charge in the profit and loss account is the dividend declared for the year:			
10	4p per share	Interim	4.4p per share	20
18	7p per share	Final	8.8p per share	40
28	11p per share	Total	13.2p per share	60
	(250)	(No. of shares)	(450)	

	b. The actual payment in the cash flow statement is made up as follows:	
	Amount owing at start of year (see balance sheet)	
16	Dividend payable	18
28	Add amount declared for the year as above	60
44		78
	Deduct amount still owing at end of year	
18	Dividend payable	40
26	Equals dividend paid (see cash flow statement)	38
26.0p	5. Earnings per Share	18.2p
65 ÷ 250	This is the profit attributable to Typical Products Ltd. shareholders divided by the number of shares	82 ÷ 450
—	6. Premium on issue of new shares	100

This is the "profit" on issue of 200 new £1 ordinary shares @ £1.50 each: i.e. 200 × 50p

7. Fixed assets

The movement on tangible fixed assets during this year is as follows:

Balance sheet value at end of last year		262
Add purchases (i.e. capital expenditure)		229
		491
Deduct sale of fixed assets	23	
depreciation	38	61
Balance sheet value at end of this year		430

262	8. Stocks and work in progress	703

Have been consistently valued at the lower of cost or estimated realizable values. Cost includes materials and, where appropriate, direct labour and production overhead and is determined on the FIFO (first in first out) basis.

250	9. Called up share capital	450

a. This represents ordinary shares of £1 each allotted and fully paid.

b. During the year an additional 200 shares were issued by rights issue @ £1.50 each; the resulting share premium has been transferred to reserves.

10. Accounting Convention

The accounts have been prepared under the historical cost convention and therefore the impact of inflation has not been taken into account.

APPENDIX C

Extracts from the Published Annual Report and Accounts Booklet of John Waddington PLC for the year ended 3 April 1993

Notes:

1. These pages are reproduced simply as an example of good practice and no further comment will be made upon them.

2. The reader is invited to note the difference between the hypothetical Appendix B and the real example herewith.

3. Note in particular the very many notes which are required in practice to support a set of published accounts.

4. Note the statement of accounting policies on page 216.

The author wishes to thank John Waddington PLC for permission to reproduce.

Report of the Auditors
to the Members of John Waddington PLC appears at page 229.

John Waddington PLC	Consolidated profit and loss account

for the financial year ended 3 April 1993

	Notes	1993 £000	1992 £000
Turnover	1	221,556	231,386
Costs and overheads	2	203,397	215,517
Operating profit	1	18,159	15,869
Loss on sale of operations	4	9,000	5,307
Profit on disposal of property		—	(252)
Profit on ordinary activities before interest		9,159	10,814
Interest payable	5	3,108	3,610
Profit before taxation		6,051	7,204
Taxation	6	3,477	3,253
Profit attributable to shareholders		2,574	3,951
Dividends	7	6,355	6,325
Deficit retained		(3,781)	(2,374)
Earnings per ordinary share	8	3.19p	4.93p
Earnings per ordinary share excluding loss on sale	8	13.71p	11.60p

Statement of retained profits

	Notes	1993	1992
Profit and loss account at 5 April 1992		41,317	42,015
Deficit retained		(3,781)	(2,374)
Exchange adjustments		2,049	8
Goodwill written back on disposals	17	930	1,668
Profit and loss account at 3 April 1993		40,515	41,317

John Waddington PLC | Balance sheets

at 3 April 1993

	Notes	Group 1993 £000	Group 1992 £000	Company 1993 £000	Company 1992 £000
Fixed assets					
Tangible assets	9	87,235	84,929	27,684	28,470
Investments	10	—	—	38,187	39,277
		87,235	84,929	65,871	67,747
Current assets					
Stocks	11	28,165	25,700	16,431	15,213
Debtors	12	42,852	43,673	24,416	25,073
Cash at bank and in hand	13	14,358	10,545	9,282	10,200
		85,375	79,918	50,129	50,486
Creditors (due within one year)					
Borrowings	14	15,173	9,299	11,162	7,375
Other creditors	15	50,055	50,469	26,771	28,887
		65,228	59,768	37,933	36,262
Net current assets		20,147	20,150	12,196	14,224
Total assets less current liabilities		107,382	105,079	78,067	81,971
Creditors (due after one year)					
Borrowings	14	25,945	30,409	23,624	26,153
Other creditors		825	829	—	—
		26,770	31,238	23,624	26,153
Provisions for liabilities and charges					
Provision for loss on sale of operations		8,070	—	8,070	—
Deferred taxation	6	3,363	4,554	1,770	2,370
		11,433	4,554	9,840	2,370
Net assets	1	69,179	69,287	44,603	53,448
Capital and reserves					
Called up share capital	16	20,669	20,534	20,669	20,534
Share premium account	17	1,818	1,052	1,818	1,052
Capital reserve	17	6,177	6,384	6,177	6,384
Profit and loss account	18	40,515	41,317	15,939	25,478
		69,179	69,287	44,603	53,448

V H Watson
D G Perry
Directors
Approved by the Board
on 29 June 1993

John Waddington PLC	Cash flow statement

for the financial year ended 3 April 1993

	Notes	1993 £000	1992 £000
Net inflow from operating activities	19	22,873	32,135
Returns on investments and servicing of finance			
Interest received		187	127
Interest paid		(3,285)	(4,487)
Dividends paid		(6,333)	(6,313)
Net outflow from returns on investments and servicing of finance		(9,431)	(10,673)
Taxation			
UK Corporation tax paid		(2,350)	(2,566)
Overseas tax paid		(908)	(757)
Tax paid		(3,258)	(3,323)
Investing activities			
Purchase of tangible assets		(9,606)	(17,402)
Purchase of subsidiaries (net of cash acquired)		—	147
Payment of deferred consideration for acquisitions		—	(440)
Sale of tangible assets		509	1,922
Disposal of subsidiary	20	254	2,418
Repayment of purchase consideration		—	441
Goodwill on acquisition of businesses		(207)	—
Net outflow from investing activities		(9,050)	(12,914)
Net inflow before financing		1,134	5,225
Financing	21		
Issue of ordinary shares		(901)	(494)
New loans		(6,068)	(13,470)
Repayment of loans		4,750	9,194
Net cash inflow from financing		(2,219)	(4,770)
Increase in cash and cash equivalents	22	3,353	9,995
		1,134	5,225

John Waddington PLC	Statement of total recognised gains

for the financial year ended 3 April 1993

	1993 £000	1992 £000
Profit attributable to shareholders	2,574	3,951
Currency translation differences	2,049	8
Goodwill written back on disposals	930	5,792
	5,553	9,751

There is no material difference between the results as disclosed in the profit and loss account and the results on a historical cost basis.

Reconciliation of movement in shareholders' funds

for the financial year ended 3 April 1993

	1993 £000	1992 £000
Profit attributable to shareholders	2,574	3,951
Dividends	6,355	6,325
	(3,781)	(2,374)
Currency translation differences	2,049	8
New share capital issued	901	494
Goodwill written off	(207)	(164)
Repayment of purchase consideration	—	841
Goodwill written back on disposals	930	5,792
	(108)	4,597
Shareholders' funds at start of year	69,287	64,690
Shareholders' funds at end of year	69,179	69,287

John Waddington PLC | Notes to the accounts

Accounting policies

General

The group accounts are prepared in accordance with applicable accounting standards, including FRS 3, under the historical cost convention as modified by the revaluation of certain assets and consolidate the accounts of the holding company and subsidiaries on the basis of audited accounts made up to the Saturday falling within the period from 29 March to 4 April each year.

Turnover

Turnover represents amounts invoiced to external customers, excluding value added tax.

Tangible assets

Tangible assets in the accounts of each company within the group are stated at cost to the group, except in the case of certain assets which have been revalued, less aggregate depreciation.

Depreciation

The charge is calculated at rates appropriate to write off the cost or valuation of individual assets from the time they become operational by equal annual instalments over their estimated useful lives which are principally as follows:

Freehold buildings — 25 or 50 years
Leasehold property — Period of lease
Plant, equipment and motor vehicles — 4 to 10 years
Freehold land is not depreciated.

Goodwill

The amount by which the fair value of the consideration on the acquisition of a business exceeds the fair value of its net assets is written off against reserves. Upon disposal of previously acquired businesses goodwill written off is reinstated in ascertaining the profit or loss on disposal.

Stocks

Stocks are stated at the lower of cost and net realisable value. Cost includes appropriate overheads and is determined on the "first in first out" or average cost basis.

Deferred taxation

No provision is made for deferred taxation unless there is a reasonable probability of payment in the foreseeable future.

Rates of exchange

Assets and liabilities expressed in overseas currencies are translated into sterling at the exchange rates ruling at the balance sheet date and trading results at average rates during the year.

Exchange gains or losses of a trading nature are dealt with in the profit and loss account; other gains or losses and translation differences are taken directly to reserves.

Research and development

All such expenditure is written off in the year in which it is incurred.

Capitalisation of interest

Tangible assets include amounts in respect of interest paid on borrowings related to the financing of major projects during their period of construction.

Pension costs

The cost of providing pension benefits is charged to the profit and loss account over the period benefiting from employees' services.

| John Waddington PLC | Notes to the accounts (continued) |

1. Segment information		Turnover		Operating profit		Assets employed	
		1993 £000	1992 £000	1993 £000	1992 £000	1993 £000	1992 £000
By class of business:							
Packaging		125,573	125,723	12,256	10,040	77,397	77,242
Specialist printing		49,577	42,875	4,283	4,001	13,026	12,208
Games		25,790	25,897	3,426	3,421	9,495	10,933
Continuing operations		200,940	194,495	19,965	17,462	99,918	100,383
Operations sold		20,616	36,891	(1,806)	(1,593)	7,590	9,470
		221,556	231,386	18,159	15,869	107,508	109,853
By location of customer:							
United Kingdom		149,783	166,134				
Europe		25,006	23,591				
USA		40,029	37,556				
Rest of world		6,738	4,105				
		221,556	231,386				
By origin:							
United Kingdom		143,019	143,101	15,031	12,210	66,785	80,761
Europe		17,959	14,538	1,087	951	6,875	3,283
USA		39,962	36,856	3,847	4,301	26,258	16,339
Continuing operations		200,940	194,495	19,965	17,462	99,918	100,383
Operations sold		20,616	36,891	(1,806)	(1,593)	7,590	9,470
		221,556	231,386	18,159	15,869	107,508	109,853

Assets employed reconcile to the group balance sheet as follows:	1993	1992
Assets employed	107,508	109,853
Finance debt less cash at bank and in hand	(26,760)	(29,163)
Current and deferred taxation	(8,116)	(7,972)
Dividends	(3,453)	(3,431)
Net assets	69,179	69,287

John Waddington PLC	Notes to the accounts (continued)

2. Costs and overheads		1993 £000	1992 £000
	Change in stocks of finished goods and work in progress	(2,156)	(1,746)
	Own work capitalised	(390)	(164)
	Other operating income	(1,855)	(1,593)
	Raw materials and consumables	89,363	100,022
	Other external and operating charges	44,669	44,655
	Staff costs (Note 3)	62,952	64,004
	Depreciation	10,814	10,339
		203,397	215,517
	Other external and operating charges include:		
	Redundancy and reorganisation costs	808	2,463
	Auditors' remuneration	217	215
	Auditors' remuneration for non-audit work	208	168
	Hire of plant and equipment	970	986
	Profit on sale of tangible assets	(124)	(392)
	Research and development	1,869	1,924

3. Employees and directors		1993 £000	1992 £000
	Staff costs:		
	Wages and salaries	55,425	56,495
	Social security costs	6,099	5,961
	Other pension costs (Note 23)	1,428	1,548
		62,952	64,004
	The average number of persons employed by the group during the year was:	Number of employees	
	United Kingdom	2,692	2,928
	Rest of world	794	740
		3,486	3,668
	The emoluments of the directors of the company included above were as follows:	£000	£000
	Fees	30	26
	Management remuneration including pension contributions	496	465
	Performance related payments	181	—
	Compensation for loss of office	—	80
		707	571

John Waddington PLC | Notes to the accounts (continued)

3. Employees and directors
(continued)

The remuneration of the executive directors is determined by a Remuneration Committee of the board, the members of which are non-executive directors. Executive directors are entitled to a performance-related payment based upon the improvement in underlying earnings.

Directors' emoluments, excluding pension contributions

Chairman:

Salary	49	45
Value of benefits in kind	6	5
	55	50

Highest paid:

Salary	149	145
Performance related payments	67	—
Value of benefits in kind	6	4
	222	149

Other directors:

	Number of directors	
	1993	1992
£10,001 – £15,000	2	2
£25,001 – £30,000	—	1
£100,001 – £105,000	—	1
£125,001 – £130,000	—	1
£170,001 – £175,000	1	—
£220,001 – £225,000	1	—

4. Loss on sale of operations

	1993	1992
	£000	£000
Loss (profit) on disposal	8,070	(485)
Goodwill previously written off to capital reserve (Note 17)	930	5,792
	9,000	5,307

On 23 June 1993 contracts were exchanged for the sale to Adare Printing Group PLC of the business and certain assets of Waddingtons Business Forms Limited for a cash consideration of £1,316,000, of which £500,000 is payable on completion and the remainder over the next five years.

Full provision has been made in these accounts for the estimated loss on disposal. Completion of the sale is conditional on the approval of the transaction at an Extraordinary General Meeting of the shareholders of Adare on 16 July 1993.

| John Waddington PLC | Notes to the accounts (continued) |

5. Interest payable

	1993 £000	1992 £000
Interest payable on:		
Debentures	92	93
Bank loans	2,884	3,224
Bank overdrafts	246	902
Other	73	141
Interest receivable on:		
Short term deposits and bank balances	(187)	(127)
	3,108	4,233
Interest capitalised	—	(623)
	3,108	3,610

6. Taxation

	1993 £000	1992 £000
Based on profits for the year:		
UK corporation tax at 33%	3,645	1,337
Overseas taxation	1,023	725
Deferred taxation	(1,191)	1,191
	3,477	3,253

The tax charge has been reduced by £540,000 (1992 £900,000) in respect of overseas trading and £NIL (1992 £100,000) because of rollover relief available on capital gains.

The potential liability at 33% for deferred taxation is as follows:

	Amount provided		Potential	
	1993 £000	1992 £000	1993 £000	1992 £000
Group				
Accelerated capital allowances	3,886	4,170	8,504	7,805
Other timing differences	(523)	384	(523)	578
	3,363	4,554	7,981	8,383

The movement in the amount provided includes a reduction of £600,000 in respect of the sale of operations.

	1993 £000	1992 £000	1993 £000	1992 £000
Company				
Accelerated capital allowances	2,284	2,370	3,625	4,743
Other timing differences	(514)	—	(514)	100
	1,770	2,370	3,111	4,843

John Waddington PLC | Notes to the accounts (continued)

7. Dividends

	1993 £000	1992 £000
Ordinary		
Interim of 3.6p per share (1992 3.6p)	2,874	2,866
Proposed final of 4.3p per share (1992 4.3p)	3,453	3,431
	6,327	6,297
Preference	28	28
	6,355	6,325

8. Earnings per ordinary share

	1993 £000	1992 £000
Earnings per share are calculated as follows:		
Profit after taxation	2,574	3,951
Preference dividends	28	28
	2,546	3,923
Earnings per share	3.19p	4.93p

Earnings per share excluding loss on sale of operations are also presented in order to give an indication of the underlying performance of the group and are calculated as follows:

	1993	1992
Profit after taxation	2,574	3,951
Preference dividends	28	28
	2,546	3,923
Loss on sale of operations	9,000	5,307
Taxation on loss on sale of operations	(600)	—
	10,946	9,230
Earnings per share excluding loss on sale of operations	13.71p	11.60p

Both calculations of earnings per share are based on the average number of ordinary shares in issue during the year ranking for dividend of 79,837,953 (1992 79,573,128).

9. Tangible assets

£000	Freehold property	Short leasehold property	Plant and vehicles	Other equipm't	Total
Group					
Cost or valuation					
5 April 1992	35,736	1,169	84,347	15,924	137,176
Exchange adjustments	1,128	109	1,536	1,537	4,310
Subsidiary disposed of	(231)	—	(1,480)	(97)	(1,808)
Additions	70	9	9,531	2,326	11,936
Disposals	—	—	(2,006)	(766)	(2,772)
3 April 1993	36,703	1,287	91,928	18,924	148,842
Being: Cost	31,367	1,287	91,928	18,924	143,506
Valuation 1977	306	—	—	—	306
Valuation 1980	5,030	—	—	—	5,030

John Waddington PLC | Notes to the accounts (continued)

9. Tangible assets (continued)

Aggregate Depreciation

	Freehold	Short leasehold	Plant and vehicles	Other equip't	Total
5 April 1992	2,807	120	39,459	9,861	52,247
Exchange adjustments	108	—	836	763	1,707
Subsidiary disposed of	(22)	—	(676)	(76)	(774)
Disposals	—	—	(1,720)	(667)	(2,387)
Charge for year	613	68	7,450	2,683	10,814
3 April 1993	3,506	188	45,349	12,564	61,607

Net book amounts

	Freehold	Short leasehold	Plant and vehicles	Other equip't	Total
3 April 1993	33,197	1,099	46,579	6,360	87,235
4 April 1992	32,929	1,049	44,888	6,063	84,929

£000	Freehold property	Short leasehold property	Plant and vehicles	Other equipm't	Total
Company					
Cost or valuation					
5 April 1992	2,953	—	47,392	3,691	54,036
Additions	—	—	3,847	531	4,378
Disposals	—	—	(1,911)	(275)	(2,186)
3 April 1993	2,953	—	49,328	3,947	56,228
Being: Cost	547	—	49,328	3,947	53,822
Valuation 1977	306	—	—	—	306
Valuation 1980	2,100	—	—	—	2,10.
Aggregate Depreciation					
5 April 1992	608	—	22,556	2,402	25,566
Disposals	—	—	(1,509)	(97)	(1,606)
Charge for year	16	—	4,171	397	4,584
3 April 1993	624	—	25,218	2,702	28,544
Net book amounts					
3 April 1993	2,329	—	24,110	1,245	27,684
4 April 1992	2,345	—	24,836	1,289	28,470

Freehold property includes £1,307,000 (1992 £1,307,000) in respect of interest capitalised.

| John Waddington PLC | Notes to the accounts (continued) |

9. Tangible assets (continued)

On a historical cost basis freehold property would have been stated at:

	Group		Company	
	1993 £000	1992 £000	1993 £000	1992 £000
Cost	33,436	32,675	1,439	1,415
Aggregate depreciation	3,126	2,616	394	380
Net book amount	30,310	30,059	1,045	1,035

Future capital expenditure not provided in the accounts:

	Group		Company	
Contracts placed	1,332	6,399	482	1,616
Authorised by the directors but for which contract not yet placed	588	2,172	377	324
	1,920	8,571	859	1,940

10. Investments

	Shares £000	Loans £000	Prov'ns £000	Total £000
Subsidiaries				
5 April 1992	43,686	14,345	(18,754)	39,277
Movement during year	39,805	(15,793)	(25,102)	(1,090)
3 April 1993	83,491	(1,448)	(43,856)	38,187

The principal operating companies of the group are shown on page 32*.

11. Stocks

	Group		Company	
	1993 £000	1992 £000	1993 £000	1992 £000
Raw materials	8,884	8,329	4,856	4,977
Work in progress	5,666	5,392	4,768	3,964
Finished goods	13,615	11,979	6,807	6,272
	28,165	25,700	16,431	15,213

12. Debtors

	1993 £000	1992 £000	1993 £000	1992 £000
Trade debtors	36,458	37,985	17,954	20,013
Other debtors	2,086	2,891	1,283	1,250
Prepayments and accrued income	4,308	2,797	2,758	1,768
Amounts owed by group companies	—	—	2,421	2,042
	42,852	43,673	24,416	25,073

*Not reproduced

John Waddington PLC | **Notes to the accounts (continued)**

13. Cash at bank and in hand

	Group 1993 £000	Group 1992 £000	Company 1993 £000	Company 1992 £000
Short term deposits	7,954	3,872	7,907	3,858
Cash and bank balances	6,404	6,673	1,375	6,342
	14,358	10,545	9,282	10,200

14. Borrowings

	Group 1993	Group 1992	Company 1993	Company 1992
Secured				
10$^{1}/_{2}$% Debenture stock 1990/95	878	878	878	878
Bank loans in foreign currencies at floating rates on variable fixture terms	675	1,005	—	—
	1,553	1,883	878	878
Unsecured				
Bank loans in sterling at various floating rates and fixture terms	21,972	22,985	21,597	22,118
Bank loans in foreign currencies at various floating rates and fixture terms	16,732	14,439	9,856	8,175
Bank overdrafts	861	401	2,455	2,357
	41,118	39,708	34,786	33,528
Repayable				
Over five years	418	3,109	—	2,800
Between two and five years	14,628	17,250	13,548	16,185
Between one and two years	10,899	10,050	10,076	7,168
	25,945	30,409	23,624	26,153
Within one year	15,173	9,299	11,162	7,375
	41,118	39,708	34,786	33,528

The debenture stock is secured by a first floating charge on the undertaking, property and assets of the company. In accordance with the Trust Deed the company has given notice to holders of the stock that it will redeem at par on 30 June 1993 and cancel all the nominal amount of the stock outstanding and registered at that date.

The bank loans in foreign currencies of certain overseas subsidiaries are secured on the current assets of those subsidiaries.

| John Waddington PLC | Notes to the accounts (continued) |

15. Other creditors (due within one year)

	Group		Company	
	1993 £000	1992 £000	1993 £000	1992 £000
Trade creditors	26,366	28,302	13,792	14,419
Corporation tax	4,753	3,418	1,560	1,228
Social security and taxation	3,898	3,889	2,471	2,657
Accruals and deferred income	6,035	6,101	2,141	2,210
Dividends	3,453	3,431	3,453	3,431
Amounts due to group companies	—	—	905	1,530
Other creditors	5,550	5,328	2,449	3,412
	50,055	50,469	26,771	28,887

16. Called up share capital

	Authorised		Allotted and fully paid	
	1993 £000	1992 £000	1993 £000	1992 £000
5.6% Cumulative preference shares of £1 each	200	200	200	200
4.2% Cumulative preference shares of £1 each	500	500	401	401
Ordinary shares of 25p each	27,000	27,000	20,068	19,933
	27,700	27,700	20,669	20,534

Shares allotted during the year:	Number	Nominal Value £000	Net Consideration £000
On exercise of options	538,130	135	901

Under share option schemes, share options outstanding at 3 April 1993 to subscribe for ordinary shares of 25p each were as follows:

Number	Price per Share	Exercisable
52,677	168.0p – 177.0p	1993
108,000	153.5p	between 1993 and 1994
145,558	175.5p – 197.5p	between 1993 and 1998
190,000	182.2p	between 1993 and 1999
897,000	134.8p – 153.5p	between 1993 and 2000
102,485	177.0p	1994
170,000	181.5p – 199.0p	between 1994 and 2001
94,150	168.0p	1995
540,000	178.0p – 181.5p	between 1995 and 2002
968,581	177.0p	1997

| John Waddington PLC | Notes to the accounts (continued) | | |

17. Reserves

	1993	1992
	£000	£000
Share premium account		
5 April 1992	1,052	645
Arising on exercise of options in year	766	407
3 April 1993	1,818	1,052
Capital reserve		
5 April 1992	6,384	1,583
Repayment of purchase consideration	—	841
Goodwill arising on acquisitions	(207)	(164)
Disposal of operations:		
Reinstatement of goodwill previously written off against capital reserve	930	5,792
Goodwill written back to profit and loss account	(930)	(1,668)
3 April 1993	6,177	6,384

The cumulative amount of goodwill charged to group reserves at 3 April 1993, net of goodwill attributable to subsidiaries subsequently sold, is £45,254,000 (1992 £45,977,000).

18. Profit and loss account

John Waddington PLC has not presented its own profit and loss account as permitted by Section 230 of the Companies Act 1985. The amount of the consolidated profit for the financial year dealt with in the profit and loss account of the holding company is shown below:

	£000
5 April 1992	25,478
Loss for year	(2,979)
Dividends	(6,355)
Exchange loss	(1,135)
Goodwill written back on disposal	930
3 April 1993	15,939

19. Cash flow from operating activities

	1993	1992
	£000	£000
Operating profit	18,159	15,869
Depreciation	10,814	10,339
Profit on sale of tangible assets	(124)	(392)
(Increase) decrease in stocks	(2,805)	117
Decrease in debtors	499	3,184
(Decrease) increase in creditors	(3,116)	3,069
Exchange differences	(554)	(51)
Net inflow from operating activities	22,873	32,135

| John Waddington PLC | Notes to the accounts (continued) |

20. Disposal of subsidiary

	1993	1992
	£000	£000
Net assets disposed of:		
Tangible assets	1,034	2,689
Stocks	340	976
Debtors	509	3,109
Cash at bank and in hand	309	—
Creditors	(999)	(4,675)
Bank loans	(368)	—
Taxation	(75)	—
Deferred taxation	—	(166)
Net assets disposed of	750	1,933
Profit on disposal	—	485
Proceeds of disposal	750	2,418
Satisfied by:		
Cash	563	2,418
Deferred consideration	187	—
	750	2,418
Net inflow of cash:		
Cash consideration	563	2,418
Cash at bank and in hand disposed of	(309)	—
Net inflow of cash in respect of disposal of subsidiary	254	2,418

On 22 April 1992 Gilmour & Dean Limited was sold for a total consideration of £750,000.

21. Analysis of changes in financing

	Share capital and premium	Bank loans and debentures
	£000	£000
5 April 1992	21,586	39,307
Share options exercised	901	—
New loans	—	6,068
Repayment of loans	—	(4,750)
Loans of subsidiary disposed of during the year	—	(368)
3 April 1993	22,487	40,257

| John Waddington PLC | Notes to the accounts (continued) |

22. Cash and cash equivalents

	Cash at bank and in hand £000	Bank overdrafts £000	1993 Total £000	1992 Total £000
5 April 1992	10,545	(401)	10,144	149
Movement in year	3,813	(460)	3,353	9,995
3 April 1993	14,358	(861)	13,497	10,144

23. Pension commitments

The group operates a number of pension schemes in the United Kingdom. The three principal schemes are funded defined benefit schemes. The assets of these schemes are held under trust and are managed by outside investment managers.

The contributions to the principal schemes are determined by a qualified actuary on the basis of triennial valuations using the projected unit method. The most recent actuarial valuations for the principal schemes were carried out at different dates between 6 April 1991 and 1 October 1992.

The actuarial assumptions which have the most significant effect on the results of the valuations are those relating to the rate of return on investments and the rates of increase in earnings and pensions. The principal assumptions used in the actuarial valuations referred to above were that the average long-term investment returns would exceed increases in earnings by 1.5% and that increases in pensions will be in line with the average rate of increase paid in recent years.

The last actuarial valuations showed that, at the different valuation dates, the combined market value of the schemes was £47,187,000 and the actuarial value of the assets represented 116% of the benefits that had accrued to members after allowing for expected future increases in earnings. The excess value of the assets is being spread over the average remaining period of membership of current employees.

The pension cost for the year equates to the contributions made to all schemes.

24. Contingent liabilities

The company has given guarantees in respect of the indebtedness of certain group companies.

| **John Waddington PLC** | Report of the auditors |

to the members of John Waddington PLC

We have audited the accounts on pages 212 to 228 in accordance with Auditing Standards

In our opinion the accounts give a true and fair view of the state of affairs of the company and the group at 3 April 1993 and of the profit and cash flows of the group for the financial year then ended and have been properly prepared in accordance with the Companies Act 1985.

Price Waterhouse
Chartered Accountants
and Registered Auditor
9 Bond Court,
Leeds LS1 2SN

29 June 1993

Five Year Review

£000	1993	1992	1991	1990	1989
Sales	221,556	231,386	227,602	238,192	207,116
Profit before exceptional items and tax	15,051	12,511	16,027	17,607	20,136
Profit before tax	6,051	7,204	16,027	12,610	18,238
Profit after tax	2,574	3,951	11,733	9,182	13,244
Dividends	6,355	6,325	6,303	6,286	5,761
Capital expenditure	11,936	15,903	25,028	22,207	19,042
Depreciation	10,814	10,339	9,132	9,113	7,472
Average number of employees in the United Kingdom	2,692	2,928	3,165	3,665	3,522
Pence per ordinary share					
Earnings	3.19	4.93	14.75	11.59	17.03
Earnings before exceptional items	13.71	11.60	14.75	16.29	18.83
Dividend	7.90	7.90	7.90	7.90	7.30

John Waddington PLC	Supplementary consolidated profit and loss account

for the financial year ended 3 April 1993

	1993 £000	1992 £000
Turnover	221,556	231,386
Costs and overheads	203,397	213,054
Operating profit	18,159	18,332
Exceptional items	—	2,211
Interest payable	3,108	3,610
Profit before taxation	15,051	12,511
Taxation	4,077	3,253
Profit after taxation before extraordinary item	10,974	9,258
Extraordinary item	8,400	5,307
Profit for year	2,574	3,951
Dividends	6,355	6,325
Deficit retained	(3,781)	(2,374)
Earnings per ordinary share	13.71p	11.60p

Segment information

	Turnover		Operating profit	
	1993 £000	1992 £000	1993 £000	1992 £000
By class of business:				
Packaging	125,573	125,723	12,256	11,475
Specialist printing	49,577	42,875	4,283	4,001
Games	25,790	25,897	3,426	3,421
Continuing operations	200,940	194,495	19,965	18,897
Operations sold	20,616	36,891	(1,806)	(565)
	221,556	231,386	18,159	18,332

Note

The above supplementary consolidated profit and loss account and segment information has been prepared using existing accounting standards in order to facilitate comparison with historic and projected financial performance.

APPENDIX D

The Use of Discount Tables

THE PRESENT Value Table, or Discount Table, reproduced on page 233 is simply a *compound interest table in reverse*. Look at any item down the 10 percent column: the line above it will be 10 percent higher.

A compound interest table starts with a present value of £1 and accumulates forward through time to arrive at a future sum: the greater the rate of interest or the longer the time, the larger the future sum will be, and vice versa.

A present value table starts with a future sum of £1 and compounds backwards (i.e. discounts) through time to arrive at a present value: the greater the rate of interest or the longer the time, the smaller the present value will be, and vice versa. So the present value of a future sum is the amount which, if invested now at a specified rate of compound interest, will accumulate to that future sum at the end of the given period of time. Or put another way, the present value of a future sum is the most you ought to invest now for the right to receive that future sum at the given future time. Clearly the present value of any future sum must be smaller the greater the rate of compound interest required.

For example: with compound interest of 10 percent p.a., the most I ought to invest now for the right to receive £1 in 5 years time is £0.621 (look at the present value table 5 year line, 10 percent column); however if I am looking for 20 percent p.a. compound interest, then the most I ought to invest now is £0.402 (5 year line, 20 percent column).

The present value table relates to just £1 of future income; hence, with compound interest at 10 percent, the most I ought to invest now for the right to receive £2496 in 5 years time is £2496 × 0.621 or £1550.

With compound interest of 15 percent, what is the most that I ought to invest now for the right to receive the following package of future sums: £100 after one year, plus £200 after 2 years, plus £700 after 3 years, plus £800 after 4 years? The present value table is used to ascertain the answer as follows:

Year	Future sum £ a	15% discount factor b	Present value @ 15% £ c = a × b
1	100	0.870	87.0
2	200	0.756	151.2
3	700	0.658	460.6
4	800	0.572	457.6
Total	£1800		£1156.4

The reader is invited to prove that with a compound interest rate of 20 percent, the present value of the above stream of future sums falls to £1013.

Variations on the use of the present value table permit the calculation of a net present value (NPV) or an internal rate of return (IRR). These expressions are described in Chapter 17.

Using slightly different words to those used elsewhere in this book, we have three significant pieces of terminology:

The *present value* of a cash inflow which is expected to be received at a specified time in the future is that amount which, if invested today at a specified compound rate of return, would accumulate to that cash inflow.

The *net present value* of a project is the difference between the present value of that project's estimated future cash inflows and the present value of its estimated investment outlay. A project is financially acceptable if its net present value is equal to, or greater than, zero at a specified compound rate of return.

The *internal rate of return* of a project is that compound rate of return which makes the net present value of a project equal zero. It is thus that compound rate of return which is offered by the project's estimated future cash inflows. (In practice the internal rate of return is found by trial and error: i.e. keep trying different rates until one is found which produces a net present value of zero.)

Present Value of £1

Years Hence	1%	2%	4%	6%	8%	10%	12%	14%	15%	16%	18%	20%	22%	25%	30%	35%	40%	50%
1	0.990	0.980	0.962	0.943	0.926	0.909	0.893	0.877	0.870	0.862	0.847	0.833	0.820	0.800	0.769	0.741	0.714	0.667
2	0.980	0.961	0.925	0.890	0.857	0.826	0.797	0.769	0.756	0.743	0.718	0.694	0.672	0.640	0.592	0.549	0.510	0.444
3	0.971	0.942	0.889	0.840	0.794	0.751	0.712	0.675	0.658	0.641	0.609	0.579	0.551	0.512	0.455	0.406	0.364	0.296
4	0.961	0.924	0.855	0.792	0.735	0.683	0.636	0.592	0.572	0.552	0.516	0.482	0.451	0.410	0.350	0.301	0.260	0.198
5	0.951	0.906	0.822	0.747	0.681	0.621	0.567	0.519	0.497	0.476	0.437	0.402	0.370	0.328	0.269	0.233	0.186	0.132
6	0.942	0.888	0.790	0.705	0.630	0.564	0.507	0.456	0.432	0.410	0.370	0.335	0.303	0.262	0.207	0.165	0.133	0.088
7	0.933	0.871	0.760	0.665	0.583	0.513	0.452	0.400	0.376	0.354	0.314	0.279	0.249	0.210	0.159	0.122	0.095	0.059
8	0.923	0.853	0.731	0.627	0.540	0.467	0.404	0.351	0.327	0.305	0.266	0.233	0.204	0.168	0.123	0.091	0.068	0.039
9	0.914	0.837	0.703	0.592	0.500	0.424	0.361	0.308	0.284	0.263	0.225	0.194	0.167	0.134	0.094	0.067	0.048	0.026
10	0.905	0.820	0.676	0.558	0.463	0.386	0.322	0.270	0.247	0.227	0.191	0.162	0.137	0.107	0.073	0.050	0.035	0.017
11	0.896	0.804	0.650	0.527	0.429	0.350	0.287	0.237	0.215	0.195	0.162	0.135	0.112	0.086	0.056	0.037	0.025	0.012
12	0.887	0.788	0.625	0.497	0.397	0.319	0.257	0.208	0.187	0.168	0.137	0.112	0.092	0.069	0.043	0.027	0.018	0.008
13	0.879	0.773	0.601	0.469	0.368	0.290	0.229	0.182	0.163	0.145	0.116	0.093	0.075	0.055	0.033	0.020	0.013	0.005
14	0.870	0.758	0.577	0.442	0.340	0.263	0.205	0.160	0.141	0.125	0.099	0.078	0.062	0.044	0.025	0.015	0.009	0.003
15	0.861	0.743	0.555	0.417	0.315	0.239	0.183	0.140	0.123	0.108	0.084	0.065	0.051	0.035	0.020	0.011	0.006	0.002
16	0.853	0.728	0.534	0.394	0.292	0.218	0.163	0.123	0.107	0.093	0.071	0.054	0.042	0.028	0.015	0.008	0.005	0.002
17	0.844	0.714	0.513	0.371	0.270	0.198	0.146	0.108	0.093	0.080	0.060	0.045	0.034	0.023	0.012	0.006	0.003	0.001
18	0.836	0.700	0.494	0.350	0.250	0.180	0.130	0.095	0.081	0.069	0.051	0.038	0.028	0.018	0.009	0.005	0.002	0.001
19	0.828	0.686	0.475	0.331	0.232	0.164	0.116	0.083	0.070	0.060	0.043	0.031	0.023	0.014	0.007	0.003	0.002	
20	0.820	0.673	0.456	0.312	0.215	0.149	0.104	0.073	0.061	0.051	0.037	0.026	0.019	0.012	0.005	0.002	0.001	
21	0.811	0.660	0.439	0.294	0.199	0.135	0.093	0.064	0.053	0.044	0.031	0.022	0.015	0.009	0.004	0.002	0.001	
22	0.803	0.647	0.422	0.278	0.184	0.123	0.083	0.056	0.046	0.038	0.026	0.018	0.013	0.007	0.003	0.001	0.001	
23	0.795	0.634	0.406	0.262	0.170	0.112	0.074	0.049	0.040	0.033	0.022	0.015	0.010	0.006	0.002	0.001		
24	0.788	0.622	0.390	0.247	0.158	0.102	0.066	0.043	0.035	0.028	0.019	0.013	0.008	0.005	0.002	0.001		
25	0.780	0.610	0.375	0.233	0.146	0.092	0.059	0.038	0.030	0.024	0.016	0.010	0.007	0.004	0.001	0.001		
26	0.772	0.598	0.361	0.220	0.135	0.084	0.053	0.033	0.026	0.021	0.014	0.009	0.006	0.003	0.001			
27	0.764	0.586	0.347	0.207	0.125	0.076	0.047	0.029	0.023	0.018	0.011	0.007	0.005	0.002	0.001			
28	0.757	0.574	0.333	0.196	0.116	0.069	0.042	0.026	0.020	0.016	0.010	0.006	0.004	0.002	0.001			
29	0.749	0.563	0.321	0.185	0.107	0.063	0.037	0.022	0.017	0.014	0.008	0.005	0.003	0.002	0.001			
30	0.742	0.552	0.308	0.174	0.099	0.057	0.033	0.020	0.015	0.012	0.007	0.004	0.003	0.001				
40	0.672	0.453	0.208	0.097	0.046	0.022	0.011	0.005	0.004	0.003	0.001	0.001						
50	0.608	0.372	0.141	0.054	0.021	0.009	0.003	0.001	0.001	0.001								

INDEX